# BEIRUT
# SCARRED CITY

Also by Beatrice Teissier and published by Signal Books:

*Into the Kazakh Steppe: John Castle's Mission to Khan Abulkhayir*
*Russian Frontiers: Eighteenth-Century British Travellers in the Caspian, Caucasus and Central Asia*

# BEIRUT
# SCARRED CITY

## WALKS THROUGH BEAUTY
## AND BRUTALISM

## BEATRICE TEISSIER

Signal Books
Oxford

First published in 2022 by
Signal Books Limited
36 Minster Road
Oxford OX4 1LY
www.signalbooks.co.uk

A catalogue record for this book is available from the British Library

ISBN 978-1-8384630-3-8 paper

Cover Design: Tora Kelly
Typesetting: Tora Kelly
Cover Image: Beatrice Teissier (front); Billy Barraclough (back)
Photos: Beatrice Teissier
Map: Stephanie Ferguson
Printed in India by Imprint Press

# CONTENTS

V

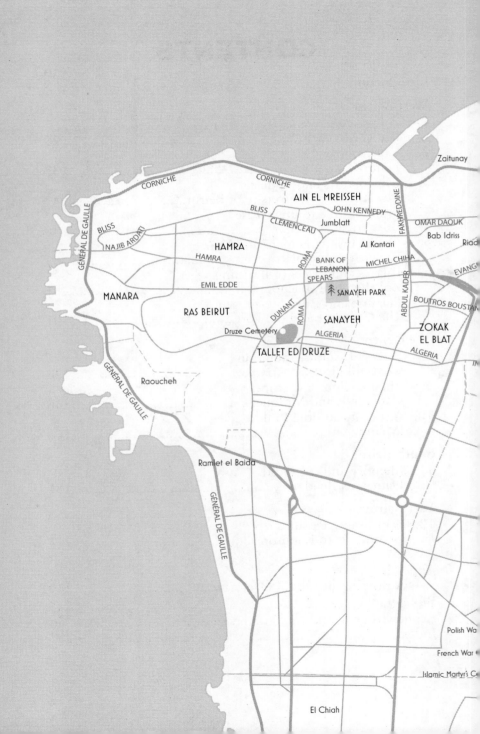

# INTRODUCTION

BEIRUT IS A SCARRED CITY. It has been disfigured many times, by earthquakes, famine, war, invasion, colonialism, foreign interference, wanton destruction, neglect and corruption. Its scars are to its fabric and to its psyche. This book hopes to contribute to the rediscovery of Beirut after its most recent disaster: the massive explosion at the port on 4 August 2020 which devastated areas of the city, obliterated the lives of many and left its citizens, already experiencing a debilitating economic crisis, enraged and traumatized. Covid-19 became almost a footnote in the lives of many. But this is not a book about trauma, it is a book about commemorating the city and the lives of its citizens.

Why would anyone want to visit Beirut after such a tragedy, given its history of conflict and reputation for gross governmental corruption, some may ask? The clichés about Beirut being the Paris, Switzerland, Monaco (and Hanoi) of the Middle East are long gone and so has much of the charm shown in late nineteenth- and early twentieth-century depictions of the city and its environs. But, as I discovered after a series of visits in 2019 and 2021, Beirut, even in crisis, has a great deal more to offer than the delicious food and the permissive nightlife that used to attract tourists in the region. The uniform, state-of-the-art modernity and ahistoricism suggested by parts of its high-rise cityscape are in large part an illusion. The fabric of the city, damaged and sometimes dilapidated, is based on a unique historical and intellectual heritage which distinguishes it from its neighbours. This is obvious in parts, hidden in others, and is best discovered by walking, as is the resilience and warmth of its people.

I originally came to Beirut to learn elementary Arabic and feeling rather claustrophobic in my immediate west Beirut neighbourhood (despite its closeness to the Corniche) and unwilling to be stuck in traffic glutted streets or be transported across the ugly highways that dissect the city and are a defining characteristic of modern Beirut, I started to walk outside my comfort zone. I preferred this option to the guided walks, both actual and virtual, round the 'sites' of Beirut (for example, the centre, the Green Line, the archaeological zone) because I wanted a more private experience. The two options can however complement each other. I walked first in the spirit of *flânerie*, casually meandering, looking but not asking questions. As I proceeded. I became aware of the differences in mood, social fabric and economic standing between neighbourhoods. I saw how one pristine pavement might immediately lead to a damaged, littered one, how decaying or restored period houses or villas are sandwiched beside huge luxury high-rises and crammed, concrete apartment blocks, how a beautiful house might be there one day and gone the next, how sandstone walls hide magnificent trees, how buildings bear the scars of war and explosion, how graffiti, street art and political flags mark territory, how street life moves from pedlars and corner coffee shops to eerie emptiness to sudden luxury or concrete barriers and razor wire, how views of the sea are few and far between, how the city seems to close in despite its hills, how asphyxiated it is by cars, how local people chat easily in English, sometimes French and mix both with Arabic, how sophisticated some people appear, or how worn down. The next corner always seemed to encourage me further. Not walking on was not an option. Yet I needed not only sensations but knowledge, and the idea for this book was born. I would write a cultural companion guide to the more easily accessible parts of this complex city - parts of central Beirut (conventionally known as west, the historic centre and east Beirut with a foray south) to which I was drawn. The book is thus not comprehensive in its coverage of the city, nor is it a guide to its world-class food and long musical traditions (covered extensively elsewhere), but rather intends to give a feel of Beirut at a particular moment in its history and of the fascinating differences between neighbourhoods and their identities.

I would record my impressions, but it would not be a personal odyssey, rather an invitation to explore and experience Beirut's diversity and historical heritage. Returning in 2021 (post-explosion and in the midst of the economic crisis) walking in Beirut was still perfectly safe.

## The city grows

As I walked in 2019 and 2021, I was struck by the strong sense of history (past and present) projected by the city's fabric. Beirut was a significant centre at different periods in its history long before it became the sophisticated, cosmopolitan and radical 1960s city of repute and the complicated, truncated, damaged metropolis of today. Its early history ranges from its first urban manifestation in the third millennium BC and the city's name, Biruta (meaning wells), appears for the first time in the second-millennium cuneiform texts of Tell Amarna and Ugarit.[1] The city became part of various ancient empires: Egyptian, Assyrian, Persian, Roman, Byzantine. After the Arab conquest of the seventh century AD, Beirut belonged to the Muslim state, succumbing to the Crusades and subsequently the Mamluks. The Ottomans then became dominant in the Levant until the end of World War I when the partitioning of the Ottoman Empire led to parts of what was known as Greater Syria (modern Syria, Lebanon, Palestine, Jordan, part of south-eastern Turkey and Iraq) passing into European control. Syria and Lebanon were mandated to the French by the League of

Nations in 1923. In Lebanon, the French Mandate lasted until after formal independence in 1943. Today what is visible from this heritage is a cat's cradle of connections which illustrate different stages in the city's development.

Beirut grew from the original old town (parts of the present centre), an irregular walled rhomboid of around five kilometres circumference, with the port projecting into the sea. By the mid to late eighteenth century the city had expanded outwards along the principal roads south (Damascus, Saida roads) and east (Propolis road) among the many cottages, orchards and mulberry plantations that surrounded the centre, with the parts between the Damascus and Saida roads filling up. The west was still very sparsely settled except for the Syrian Protestant College (later American University of Beirut), the American consulate and the St John's Hospital, mostly due to the *collines de sable* or sand dunes, where wind-blown sand was the bane of the area's inhabitants and smallholders. Except for the central Soeurs de Charité most Christian religious establishments (Greek Orthodox, Catholic etc.) were based to the south-east of the 'old town'. Consulates were mostly to the near west. Beirut's main districts, such as Ras Beirut, Achrafieh, Mazraat el-Arab (Mazra), Rumeli (Rmeil), are already named on a map of 1876 made for the Ottoman Sultan Abdul Hamid II (1842-1918).

The growth of Beirut was incremental (consular offices had already been established there in the 1820) and by the 1830s it already had a reputation for trade, but it is believed that the root of its economic prosperity and development goes back to the Egyptian occupation of 1832-40, and the efforts then made to develop the port, installing wharves and a lazaretto (quarantine facility). Road networks were improved, and streets were paved (see Zokak el Blat, p. 81). Beirut became the most important port of the region for European imports (cottons, muslins, tin, West Indian produce, hardware) and the export of Greater

Syria's goods (silk, wine, dyes, olive oil). The Ottoman Bank was established in 1850 and financiers and insurers proliferated along with real estate speculation.

In the early modern period two other major phases of urban development in the centre (superseding its original layout) stand out: when Beirut became a regional capital under Sultan Hamid in 1888, and when it became the headquarters of the French colonial government in the 1920s until the official end of the Mandate in 1946.

A hugely destructive period for Beirut's cityscape was the 1960s, when stop and start initiatives mostly based on proposals put forward by the architects and urban planners Michel Ecochard and Ernst Egli in the 1940s and early 1950s, were put into effect. A network of main thoroughfares was linked to the expanding port and the new airport, and there were other ambitious plans for green spaces, new drainage, new souks or commercial centres, and connecting roads and thoroughfares east-west and north-south. The latter were intended not only to create easier access within the city, but according to President Fouad Chehab (1902-73), to weaken the cohesiveness of confessional neighbourhoods by putting these in close contact with each other.[2] Some of these 1950s plans were still being mooted, but now including a metro network, in the 1970s to be delivered in the 1980s. Yet such utopian visions were hindered by ongoing uncontrolled development, lack of integrated policies, neighbourhoods affected by various influxes of refugees and immigrants, sectarian upheavals and then civil war.

Finally, the catastrophic port explosion in August 2020 had a profound impact on the fabric of the city: whole parts were disembowelled, other parts were left with buildings that were salvageable but with shattered windows and doors. The greater effect was on the people who were displaced, having to cope with the loss of loved ones and/or their homes.

## Crossing lines

The city is fragmented, contradictory and full of contrasts. It is demarcated not only along denominational lines, but those of family, clan, interest groups, ownership, wealth, language, race, status (citizen/ refugee) and sexuality. The first-time visitor discovers this complex stratification gradually.

The demarcation of Beirut has a long history and was (and is) at times complicated due to the streams of incomers who contributed to the overcrowding of the city and its inexorable expansion. In the early nineteenth century it had a diverse denominational population (with a Sunni majority), each part with its own quarters (as mentioned above) but with also a degree of mixing and confessional overlap due to business. Christian demarcation had been made with the settlement of the Greek Orthodox community close to their principal eighteenth-century church (St George, built on much earlier foundations) south-east of the old town. In the course of the nineteenth century influxes of Greek Orthodox families migrated close to this area, with steadily incoming Maronites to the south-central area. Jews moved out of the old town's south-west to the Wadi Abu Jamil quarter. The distinct minority Druze community had holdings in west Beirut. Foreigners gravitated to the centre or to Ras Beirut, and by the late nineteenth and early twentieth centuries Ras Beirut as well as the city centre had a mixed population and remained diverse. The south-west was essentially Sunni.

By the early twentieth century, there were three major denominational groups in Beirut: Sunni Muslims, Orthodox Christians and Maronites. As the city accommodated more people, districts grew closer together (as with the meeting of Christian Basta and Muslim Mazra'a Moussaytbeh)[3] and workplace and residence became increasingly segregated. Armenians fleeing genocide in the 1900s settled to the north-

The bustle of an early twentieth-century street scene
(Library of Congress, Washington DC)

east of the city (Karantina, Burj Hammud), Palestinians after 1948 went to Ras Beirut (and helped in the development of Hamra) or to camps to the south of the city (Sabra, Chatila). Migrating Shia Muslims or those escaping Israeli aggression from the south during the 1960s settled in the south of the city. At different times other incomers from neighbouring countries (Kurds, Christians and Muslims from Syria, Egypt and Iraq) and rural Lebanon settled mostly along denominational lines and places of origin.

As Beirut developed, settlement was also decided along wealth, class and professional lines. Thus certain quarters became (and some stayed) the domain of rich merchant families, the mixed Muslim and Christian 'aristocracy' (Zokak el Blat, Gemmayze, around the port), while professionals were to be found in Ras Beirut, artisans in, for, example, Mazra'a, the middle class in Saife (Christian) and in Bachoura and Ghalgoul (mostly Muslim). Life in the suburbs inhabited by poorer refugees and immigrants developed along very different lines from that of the cosmopolitan centre and they became worlds of their own. Some, such as Burj Hammud, developed organically and thrived, but others were riven by poverty. Social and denominational crisis, particularly within unintegrated suburbs, was never far away.

The civil war (1975-90) marked possibly the most serious turning point in the history of Beirut's fragmentation. Tensions had been longstanding between Maronite Christians and Muslims since the presence of the Palestine Liberation Organization and their militarization in Lebanon after their expulsion from Jordan in 1971 under Yasser Arafat. The state was felt to be unable, under the inept and corrupt President Suleiman Frangieh, to provide security, and new armed groups and sectarian militias emerged as a result. The war is said to have officially started in April 1975 after the Christian

Maronite Phalange attacked a bus taking Palestinians to the Tel al-Zata'ar refugee camp. The main factions in the war were Maronite Christians, the LNM (Lebanese National Movement, comprised of secular leftists and Sunni Muslims), the Shi'i Amal Movement, the PLO, the Lebanese Army, with sub-groups, and the invaders and occupiers, Israel and Syria. Syrian forces were present in Lebanon from 1976 onwards, acting against Palestinian militias and in support of Christian ones with the pretext of eventually restoring calm. They became entrenched in fighting with Israel and essentially took over Lebanon, only fully withdrawing in 2005. Israel, meanwhile, has a long history of interference in Lebanon, invading in 1978 and in 1982 besieging Beirut. Israeli forces gradually withdrew to a security zone in the south in 1985, but since then there have been multiple (and ongoing) operations, incursions, clashes and strikes, mostly with Hezbollah.

A destroyed cemetery during the civil war, 1982
(Luc Chessex/ICRC/Wikimedia Commons)

As the civil war went on splintered groups arose out of the militias. The Shi'i political group, Hezbollah, was formed in 1982, partly out of the fragmentation of the civil war, but mostly in response to the Israeli invasion of Lebanon that year. Its emphasis is primarily on resistance to Israel, and it is now a major force in Lebanon, with economic and strategic areas of control.[4]

It is arguable that before the civil war, Beirut's economy, driven by the multi-confessional centre, accommodated religious differences, but during the war divisions were not only denominational, feudal and political, but social, ethnic and economic as well.[5] During the civil war intense fragmentation became the norm; not only between east and west, but within districts as well as militias and gangs battled among themselves for control of their areas and formed enclaves.[6] And at times of crisis such as in the autumn of 2021, demarcation lines between east and west can easily be resuscitated. In support of a demonstration against a judge who had summoned two Shi'i officials over the port explosion (Hezbollah controls the port), and whom Hezbollah was trying to have removed, Hezbollah and Amal militias advanced with weapons over the old demarcation line, the Saida road, around the Tayoune roundabout, between Muslim Ghobeiri and Christian Sodeco and Furn Ech Chebbak. A furious gun battle between them and the far-right Christian militia (the Lebanese Forces, under the stewardship of Samir Geagea), ensued for several hours, leaving seven dead and many injured (see p. 207). Tensions were very high for a few days, then things returned to normal. 'This is what happens in Lebanon,' say the older generation who lived through the war.

The fragmentation of the city might be construed as a means of either forgetting the war or of remembering it, but the control of space by politics and sectarianism cannot be divorced from an extreme form of capitalism.[7] Beirut's short-lived investment bubbles and development mania reflect this phenomenon perhaps more than in most cities. The massive influx of Syrian refugees into Lebanon (over one million by 2016, 1.5 million by 2021, with a consistently high birth rate) exacerbates this problem and has had a serious destabilizing capacity. Those not in camps are found renting apartments, rooms and garages, or living rough in empty spaces and begging on the streets. They are universally resented by those who experienced the controlling Syrian occupation.

Today, historical demarcation lines are open and most areas are generally welcoming for the visitor walking in Beirut. Yet some Beirutis do not venture out of their districts except for work, study and sometimes shopping, and effectively live worlds apart from other communities. In the southern Muslim suburbs of Chiyah and Ghobeiri, for example, cafés, shopping malls and other business and leisure facilities have opened to accommodate local people, who do not feel comfortable going to the centre.[8] Equally a Hamra resident would not feel inclined to go to these areas for leisure. The role of today's city centre as a neutral and working space for all (as Burj Hammud once was), as trumpeted by Solidère, the company responsible for the redevelopment of central Beirut after the war, is regrettably questionable (see p. 130ff).

It is evident that a foreigner walking in a city as complex as Beirut cannot hope to understand how the city really functions nor fully comprehend many of its citizens' experiences. The civil war, which finished just over thirty years ago, should not of course define what Beirut is, but the conflict remains very real and present for people over a certain age both in older generations' psyche and in reminders from ever-present bullet-ridden buildings and burnt-out hotels and high-rises. The war is perhaps more anecdotal for the younger generation, who nevertheless feel its residue from their parents' and grandparents' stories and the factions that still hold power. They also obtain a terrifying taste of the recent past when local gun battles occur. Memory of the even more recent explosion is still extremely raw and lived, as people have borne daily witness to loss and destruction and to the total disregard for their wellbeing on the part of the authorities. In terms of the collective psyche, these wounds may even be greater than those inflicted by the civil war as they are inflicted by criminal negligence rather than deliberate targeting. 'We have lost our grounding', 'they have killed us,' say witnesses to the explosion. This sense of hopelessness was compounded in 2021 by the dire economic situation that has plagued the country since 2019: loss of livelihoods and savings, the constant struggle to keep things going, the rise in fuel price, the shortages, hunger for those without substantial means, the constant threat of electricity cuts (days of total blackout in 2021), the brain drain. The callousness of those in power makes ordinary people feel like hostages in their own country. A Palestinian businessman whose family lost everything in 1948, and who subsequently made a successful living in Lebanon, said he felt more anger now at this government's 'betrayal of everyone', than at the Israelis: 'they were the enemy after all'.

While the civil war engendered much art, from novels and short stories to posters[9] and graffiti, this cultural response is still emerging from the port explosion and economic free-fall, and for the non-Arabic speaker is chiefly manifested in street art, memorials and the occasional (translated) memoir.[10] The heritage and memorials of the city may mean one thing to one citizen and something else to another, and once more such differing perspectives may be a question of generation. The growing post-explosion memorials can also be a source of disagreement (see p. 122).

The city's invisible lines of disassociation are presently everywhere, and the walking visitor will experience many of these visible or felt lines in its neighbourhoods, often within metres of each other. Sectarian fragmentation is something the young are fighting against, but it will take generations, according to the young (or those who hope to remain rather than join the brain drain abroad). For the visitor, however, anonymity and/or lack of prior attachment and knowledge provide a kind of innocence which enhances walking and enables a personal relationship with place to be made. This does not mean that there cannot be sensitivity to what the city and its people have endured.

## Fumes and fuming

Walking within and between the central neighbourhoods of west and east Beirut discussed in this book (Ain el Mreisseh to Gouraud Street and environs) gives a sense not only of historical (and more recent) fractures but also of how the city's heritage connects the city and what a true melting pot the city was, despite denominational enclaves. But the city, partitioned by brutal highways, provides scant provision for the pedestrian. He or she is confronted by the tyranny of the car and generally ignored traffic lights (surreally dysfunctional in times of electricity cuts) and the distances between places appear greater because of the city's lack of pedestrian infrastructure. With the fuel shortages in 2021 some hardy types took to cycling, while taxi drivers lamented, 'We are finished, they will now start walking'. This would be funny in a place like Beirut were it not so sad.

The older generation of Beirutis fondly remember the tramway system (built c. 1908, decommissioned in 1968) and efficient buses. Today public transport consists of 'service' taxis, taxis and louche looking buses. The Lebanese government was supposedly working on a World Bank project (announced in the autumn of 2017) for a comprehensive public transport system consisting of a network of bus and rapid transit solutions to be developed in several phases for Beirut and its suburbs. But for the moment - and failing administrative miracles and a green psychic revolution in the minds of Beirutis - the car is a necessity and here to stay, even in the worst fuel crisis.

Cars are everywhere and take up a vast amount of space: on pavements, double or triple parked, waiting outside buildings, gobbling up underground car parks, crammed into small plots crawling or at a standstill in long queues or speeding when they can, paying minimal attention to red lights, when in operation. Space for the car is a priority: laissez-faire town planning and amenable building regulations has promoted the destruction of historic houses for parking lots. These may be temporary, until a better proposition comes along and the problem shifts elsewhere. It is not only the lack of decent public transport within Beirut and its suburbs, and lack of provision for pedestrians, but for the rich car mania is another outlet for consumerism and a means of display. This is evident even in times of hardship. The owners of Porsches, Alfa-Romeos, Lamborghinis, Mercedes, Land Rovers, BMWs and various SUVs wait impatiently behind tinted windows in traffic jams with vans, ancient, dented taxis and clapped-out family cars, or honk their horns furiously to be let into a gated residence's car park. Occasionally convoys of governmental black limos blast their way through the congestion, stopping for no-one. 'There go the blood suckers,' people say.

The toxic fumes, contributing to high levels of pulmonary and cardio-vascular diseases (and noxious smells), are acknowledged with a shrug of the shoulders. Extravagant thoughts of flight are probably never far from the minds of Beiruti drivers. In Rawi Hage's fable *Bird Nation*,[11] 'flocks' of people stuck in vast cars in traffic jams (also immobilized by their own size) go through a series of 'car' fads (pope-mobiles, vast American Hummer vehicles), but becoming equally frustrated, start growing feathers on their backs and take to the sky (only to be shot at by politicians).

## What's in a name?

Having experienced the fast or clogged route into town in semi-lit darkness if arriving at night (2021), the first-time visitor will usually want to consult a map before setting off on foot (or by taxi) for whatever brings him or her to Beirut. They will be presented with a cornucopia of avenue and street names mostly offering a potted history of the great and good - and not so good - of Lebanon's history and of the wider Middle East. The history of Beirut's street names goes hand in hand with the expansion of the city and who was in charge. Early European maps name the three to four principal finished roads by their destination (Route de Damas, de Saida, de Pripolis, i.e. Tripoli, east towards the river). Road names became prevalent from the early 1920s onwards and by 1945 were largely French. By the 1960 and 1970s, maps show a growing variety of names, some of which were subsequently changed. Thus a number of street names are palimpsests, reflecting anti-colonial feeling in the covering up of old imperialist references: Georges Picot (diplomat and part author of the Sykes-Picot agreement which agreed to the partition of the Ottoman Empire at the end of World War I) was changed to Omar Daouk; Perthuis (after Comte Edmond de Perthuis, who obtained the concession to build the Beirut-Damascus Road, opened in 1863) was changed to commemorate President Kennedy, and the United States as an ally. Other names celebrate 'safe' historical figures, such as the reformist Ottoman statesman (Midhat Pasha), rulers from distant history (the Ummayad Caliph Omar bin Abdul Aziz, 682-720,) the Druze Emir of Mount Lebanon Fakhr al-Din (1572-1635) and philosophers (Ibn Sinna, al-Razi, Ibn Rushd). Other names are confessional: Pierre Gemayel, Maronite founder of the right-wing Christian Phalange party; Christian saints (Mar Nqoula or Nicholas, also a place) and Jeanne d'Arc; and others reflect international contacts and/or emigration and immigration (Australia, Marseille, Armenia) and ancient history (Hiram King of Tyre; Phoenicia).

Actual reality sets in when, if the visitor asks for a taxi, the driver will not know any street names, except perhaps one of the most famous, Hamra Street. The driver will ask you for the name of a district such as Gemmayze, Raouche and Horsch, or for a location such as a souk, a square, a hotel, a museum or a famous building. Street names are now only known by a few inhabitants, mostly elderly and French-speaking. According to their religious persuasion, the older generation would most probably have had their own pre-war, unofficial names for the streets they knew,[12] and this is probably still the case in many neighbourhoods. Yet street signs exist, some the worse for wear or giving a cadastral number only, and the walking visitor needs a map.

**Get walking**

Beirut is a small city and needs to be discovered carefully. The schematic map on pp. 6-7 shows the neighbourhoods explored in this book: the aim is not to give itineraries but to suggest parts to be discovered as you come across them or deliberately seek them out after consulting the book and other guides. I made my way from west to east, with periods of respite along the Corniche, but it is equally possible to head straight to areas of obvious interest, such as Hamra, Zokak el Blat, Damascus Road, the centre, Sursock or the Corniche, and later explore adjacent areas. You may want to branch out differently (where you start to walk will be partly determined by the location of your hotel or flat) but whatever your pace and mood you are encouraged to go towards not only what you are drawn to, but towards what you may not be drawn to. You will thus experience the city's invitations and sometimes rejections and above all its multiple realities and differences. Subjects of interest such as Ottoman or Mandate period monuments, museums, cemeteries or modern, sometimes brutalist, architecture may be sought out *per se*, but this approach risks missing much.

Some visitors may be stumped by nervousness of what may await them in the city, yet the curiosity, general courtesy and good humour shown to the foreigner by Beirutis (even in times of crisis) will win you over and you will want to venture out. So you will learn to circumvent the main highways, walk into the road with a hand held up to stem the flow of traffic (as done locally), simply follow hardier road-crossers or weave in and out of stationary cars. You may venture into parts that Beirutis themselves do not frequent and find yourselves, in Virginia Woolf's words (from *Street Haunting*), 'an untethered mind'. You will become aware that a watchful preparedness is part of the city's mood, particularly in recent times, and you will not want to ignore barriers, checkpoints or the requests of the police or security guards. And in order not to create offence by appearing to be a sensation-seeking visitor, you will not gape at damage, nor venture into the far southern suburbs or refugee areas without a local who can act as a guide. The visitor will surely be impressed by the ongoing post-explosion reconstruction evident in the city, despite the severe economic crisis. Mostly paid for privately or with the help of NGOs, there cannot be more of an attestation of the spirit and resilience of the people of this great stubborn city.

1   Sader 1998, 32.
2   Kassir 2011, 409-426.
3   Davie 1994, 39.
4   Daher 2016, 1.
5   Davie 1994, 50.
6   Davie 1994, 53-55.
7   Khalaf 2002, 307.
8   Arsan 2018, 359.
9   Maasri 2009. This is a study of posters produced by the different factions (e.g. Lebanese Armed Forces, communists, socialists, Amal, Islamic Resistance, later Hezbollah) across the period of the civil war. In contrast to street art, the iconography of these posters, with some exceptions, is repetitive (clenched fists, armed men, portraits, sun rays, maps). The graffiti of the period is particularly violent (cf. Maria Chakhtoura, *La guerre du graffiti*, 1978).
10  The excellent Majdalani, *Beirut 2020*.
11  *Beirut Noir*, 2015.
12  MacCarthy 1975, 83.

# BEIRUT: SCARRED CITY

# WEST BEIRUT

# 1. A LOST PORT
# AIN EL MREISSEH

HISTORICALLY DEFINED BY THE SEA and its fishermen, the area (officially Dar el Mreisseh) between Bar el Mreisseh, George Post, John Kennedy and Graham Streets encloses remnants of what used to be a very individual part of old Beirut. A map of 1876 made by the Danish diplomat Julius Loytved for Sultan Abdul Hamid II, shows almost nothing there except a few houses and orchards away from a rocky shore. Today it seems besieged by other worlds: the Corniche and luxury hotels to the east (some of which are officially part of Ain el Mreisseh) and the American University of Beirut (AUB) to the west.

The sea and fishermen were integral to this neighbourhood - essentially a fishing village - and old photographs show how the shoreline and a small fishing port reached up to what is now Dar el Mreisseh Street. These were respectively expropriated piecemeal to extend the Corniche in 1974 and by private investors to build the Al-Ahlam or 'Dreams' tower block in the 1990s (completed in 2003). Together with other residential developments, this caused the destruction of the traditional early twentieth-century sandstone houses and villas with characteristic red-tiled, pitched roofs and triple arched windows which overlooked the shore. In the 1970s the mostly Sunni and Druze fishermen strongly resisted the appropriation of the port, which had a serious impact on their livelihood, and successfully negotiated to maintain parts of it in exchange for a space to dock their boats offshore and a bridge to allow them access to the water, on condition that they evacuated their shacks. After the civil war, when land values in the area tripled, the fishermen together with conservation groups and intellectuals again protested against further government approved land-grabs, but unable to assert their rights to the port it was inevitable that the developers should win, and the Al-Ahlam tower was built. The fishing community did, however, successfully resist the idea of moving the port to Hamman al-Askari.[1] Today they are still there, albeit in much reduced numbers, their boats docked adjacent to private yacht mooring with access to the sea from under a bridge. The old beaches are back-filled, limbo-like and overgrown, and the sea hidden from eye-level. It is as if the port had never been.

According to legend, the name Ain el Mreisseh - 'spring of the (female) fishermen's chief' - was acquired when a nun who had survived a shipwreck landed on the shore and was given

Beleaguered fishing boats with underpass to the sea among restored houses and modern apartments (Beatrice Teissier)

this title once she started helping the community. Her story, with the rituals to commemorate her, are relegated to the past. The significance of the sea and memories of the neighbourhood persist, however, in a private museum established in his home (off Dar el Mreisseh) by a now deceased fisherman, Ibrahim Najem. The museum is now in the hands of his family, who are happy to receive guests and introduce them to this private cornucopia, gathered together from local donations and Najem's collecting mania. The museum resembles an overflowing cabinet of curiosities: amphorae, seashells, an early full diver's suit and helmet, fishing hooks, small antiquities, rifles, keys, padlocks, lamps, telephones, radios, irons, textiles and sandals are crammed into three rooms together with photographs of old Ain el Mreisseh and its important visitors. Najem's philosophy and that of the local, multi-denominational Ain el Mreisseh heritage group which assisted him, was that it was essential to preserve an authentic memory of the place, as all were well aware of the march of predatory developers in the area.

Ain el Mreisseh's location by the sea was always a threat to its original character. After the civil war and the rise in land value, its working-class, multi-denominational inhabitants sold to developers or were evicted, paid compensation and moved to cheaper areas, while high-rise apartments with sea views continued to be built.[2] But it was not only money that changed the character of Ain el Mreisseh: an influx of Shia escaping Israel's persecution in the south changed the social fabric of the original Sunni, Druze, Kurdish and Christian neighbourhood. During the conflict the Shia Amal and Hezbollah groups asserted control of the area, and both Sunni and Christians left. This is still quietly spoken of today.[3]

There was also a cosmopolitan side to parts of Ain el Mreisseh: the hotels such as the St George, completed in 1932, with their nightclubs on the Corniche or facing the sea to the east, attracted tourists, diplomats, journalists, artists, people from AUB and wealthy Arabs from the Gulf. This affected the locals differently: some liked the money it brought in, others, those who felt excluded, disapproved. There were particular objections by the Sunni Mosque Committee to the Hard Rock Café (1997-2013), which opened diagonally to the mosque and brought in noise and an alien clientele.

The late Ottoman-period mosque on the corner of Graham leading to the Corniche is the oldest and most historic monument of Ain el Mreisseh: it was built in from 1880 to 1887, and finished by Abdullah Beyhum on land donated by Muhammed Al-Hibri. It was one of the many mosques built during the second half of the nineteenth and early twentieth centuries as Beirut expanded to new neighbourhoods beyond the old city: these include the Ras el Naba, Al Basta, Al Fawqa, Al Kantai and Zokak el Blat mosques. This sandstone mosque is compact with a domed roof and tall minaret, but it is difficult to see it properly from the street as it is hidden by a wall. Old photos show its arched, shallow, pedimented sides and its northern entrance facing the sea. A plaque above the entrance with Koranic verses is flanked by the Ottoman symbol of crescent and star. This side is now engulfed by fumes from the double-laned freeway outside. There is another door on the east side. Renovations were carried out during the 1950s (when one door was transferred from another mosque, and another removed) and during the civil war, using reclaimed sandstone.[4] During the conflict the mosque committee was instrumental in providing assistance to the local population.[5]

The original coastline, the fishermen's port, the houses, the music and cabaret acts from the nightclubs of old are still remembered by some elderly residents, but these are not the only ghosts of the past: there are the memories of the Israeli invasion, the American Embassy, of the local theatre and of traditional houses and their gardens.

Inhabitants of the area not only heard the explosion that wrecked part of the American Embassy on the seafront in 1983, but had the glass in their windows shattered by the blast. They were to re-live this trauma with the port explosion. The 1983 bomb was a suicide mission in the name of anti-imperialist Iranian Islamic Jihad at a time when the Americans were trying to orchestrate a Middle Eastern peace plan and to negotiate for Israeli and Syrian troops to leave Lebanon. After years of provocation, Israel, with American support, had been eager to start a definitive confrontation with Lebanon, and invaded the south in 1982. Their aim was to disable the Palestine Liberation Organization (PLO), rid Lebanon of Syrian troops and establish an Israel-friendly Maronite head of state. Also landing by sea, the Israelis advanced by the coastal road with air support towards Beirut and the Beqaa Valley. They surrounded Beirut and fought the Syrians in the Beqaa. Beirut was bombed and besieged for months. As a result, and with western supervision, male PLO fighters were evacuated, and Arafat eventually established his headquarters in Tunis. The Israelis then invaded west Beirut and enabled one of the worse atrocities of the war: the slaughter of mostly civilians in the Palestinian and Lebanese Shia west Beirut refugee camps of Sabra and Chatila by Christian Phalangist militias. Locally, residents remember Israeli troops marching on the Corniche. After aborted agreements, the Israelis finally withdrew south to a 'security zone' in 1985, and only fully withdrew in 2000. Their presence is still permanently felt over Lebanese territory, however, with sonic booms from aircraft, shots fired in the south, drones and other provocations as their conflict with Hezbollah mounts in times of crisis (such as 2020-21).

A more upbeat ghost of Ain el Mreisseh takes the form of the theatre (on Graham Street). First a cinema in the 1950s, then a theatre staging western plays in 1965, during the civil war it became a locus of commemoration, ritual and political activism for various parties, from the Progressive Socialists to Hezbollah and Amal. It was then reopened as a play and film house, exhibition and conference centre in 1994, but lack of funding contributed to its closure in 2000. It remains closed and may be demolished. Such are the varied and multiple lives of many old Beirut landmarks.

Today, at first glance, this area may seem dominated by luxury and middle range high-rise apartment blocks with their small, manicured gardens, and by overcrowded 1960s concrete blocks with heavily draped balconies, as well as by abandoned buildings and others under construction. But the streets and alleyways retain a sense of scale, ownership and self-containment. For example, greengrocers, a pharmacy, small supermarkets, a mechanic's workshop, a tailor and art-framer's shop, a small art gallery, a baker, coffee-booths and a non-touristy café cater for the locals. Residents are mostly working- and middle-class Muslims and some Christians (all with Sri Lankan or Filipino maids) as well as a transient community of visitors, medical and service personnel, academics and students from AUB. The retired are still found sitting on chairs watching the world go by and original residents still meet and greet one another. The small gardens that are left on the ground or on roof terraces are private, but a few old trees survive and new ones have been planted along Dar el Mreisseh, while greenery spills over many balconies and plants fill containers in the street. The atmosphere is slightly conservative, and very different from the carnival that is the Corniche, or the melting pot of Hamra and AUB. Most of the damage from the 2020 blast has now been repaired, although the economic crisis and lack of public electricity means that shops without generators in 2021 were closed or plunged into darkness.

Doomed house on George Post Street (Beatrice Teissier)

Remnants of old Ain el Mreisseh's architecture such as houses with external staircases or sandstone walls and arched windows (usually incorporated or adjacent to a modern building) may be seen, but perhaps the most poignant of these was an arch and a vaulted space, once part of a traditional house off Van Dyck Street, which led to one of Ain el Mreisseh's derelict spaces, invaded by cats, weeds and the occasional sleeping bag. This architectural relic has now been destroyed to provide a small through road. There are cases of private restoration, like a traditional house on the left side of Dar el Mreisseh, but questions remain over heritage. For example, AUB has long extended its tentacles into Ain el Mreisseh and has now purchased a lot with a traditional house and garden on George Post Street. It has been given permission to dismantle and reassemble it at a later stage. Although activists are now involved, word has it that it may become a car park. Nevertheless, studies are being undertaken to try to maintain and revive this small part of the local heritage.[6]

1   Khalaf 1998, 155-156; Sawalha 2010, 54-57.
2   Khalaf 1998, 156; Sawalha, 2010, 65-66.
3   Sawalha 2010, 6-65.
4   Debbas 1986, 116-117, photo of 1895; from a book by Islam Chebaro, via Hayat Gebara.
5   Khalaf 1998, 156.
6   For instance, Gebara 2016.

# 2. CORNUCOPIA HAMRA

WHETHER COMING FROM OR GOING to Ain el Mreisseh, it is likely that you will use the wide Van Dyck steps (after Cornelius van Dyck, a medical doctor and missionary at the Syrian Protestant College, later the American University of Beirut, AUB). This public outdoor stairway may be your introduction to Beirut's hilly topography and are one of the more versatile and busy connections between Beirut's quartiers. Here you may find boys collecting empty cans and bottles, couples taking selfies, refugees or other destitute individuals sitting and waiting, professionals passing hurriedly talking on their phones, students from *niqab-* to Californian-clad, the odd foreigner, hungry cats, rubbish, graffiti and dog excrement.

At the head of the steps, reputedly dating from the Ottoman period, stands a decaying mansion distinguished by an arcaded gallery and triple arches with marble decoration. This is an early example of the grand style of Beiruti villas of wealthy merchants (see Zokak el Blat), and used to be surrounded by fields and orchards. The mansion was built in 1865 by the Ayas merchant family, then passed on at some point to the powerful Sinno family.[1]

Grandeur and business were combined here with the owners' shops at street level. During the civil war one floor became the Consulate General of the Philippines. The building has now been sold, and in 2019 workmen were seen there (not necessarily an optimistic sign in Beirut), but the house was still there in 2021. Immediately to the side of this mansion are some of the American University of Beirut's top of the range

Derelict property on Maamari Street (Beatrice Teissier)

medical facilities.

Once on John Kennedy the choice is to investigate the street (leading east) and to seek out early twentieth-century apartment blocks with their period facades or to turn upwards and west towards AUB and Hamra. If choosing to go towards Hamra nobody can miss the hub of people and congregation of cats around the giant baobab tree that marks one of the entrances to AUB campus. If investigating Hamra, walking down Bliss Street (named after missionary Daniel Bliss, founder and president of what became AUB) and up Jeanne D'Arc will bring you to the area whose name has associations with the Arabic word for 'red'. Given the once local reddish sand dunes and planted prickly pears as well as Hamra's eventual reputation as a hub of pleasure, the latter association is the easier to make. This is disputed.[2]

Hamra was not planned: it grew initially because of the working and educational opportunities offered by the Protestant College, the predecessor of AUB established in 1866. Old photographs show the dirt road lined by cacti that was Bliss Street when the college was first built. The area consisted of small-scale cottage gardens and farmhouses, with a few villas. It was bordered to the west by the sea and the high-end area known as Ras Beirut and to the south-east by sand dunes. Hamra never became, like the Sursock area, exclusively the domain of merchant families and their palaces, but was a mixture of the latter (Sinno, Itani, Daouk) and the residences of middle- and working-class urban and village migrants and foreigners who realized the benefits of the area and opened businesses. Space quickly came at a premium and land values rose massively. Floors were added to existing houses. In the 1950s there was a construction boom and by the 1960s the character of Hamra as a warren of disparate architecture (in which concrete blocks featured large) and as a centre for retail and international and local business was established. Traditional houses with external staircases and walled gardens disappeared.

The indigenous population of Hamra had been Greek Orthodox, Sunni and Druze. With the Protestant College came other Christians. Immigrants were added to the mix: Armenians fleeing massacres from 1914 onwards and Palestinians from the tragedy of 1948 and its aftermath arrived. The middle class with business backgrounds from these groups settled in the area and became assimilated, contributing to the development of the area, but also to its sophistication, something that was not initially approved of.[3] Capital came in from the Gulf States and Egyptian, Syrian and Jordanian migrants also came to benefit from what this part of Beirut had to offer.

Hamra and its main street gained a reputation for cosmopolitanism, café culture, cinemas and chic retail outlets. The Horseshoe Café opened in 1959 (at the base of the first glass and steel facade office building on Hamra Street built in 1958)[4] and with the Café de Paris, Wimpy, Modca and l'Express turning into artists' and students' hip places, nightlife and radical conversations thrived. The renown of Hamra survives in people's memories (and imaginations for those who have never been there) and in the civil war novels of Beirut.

The war changed everything say those who lived through it; it was then, according to some, that the demarcation between east (Christian) and west (Muslim) became official and lethal.[5] Whether the city was ever seen as a single entity is debatable, but the war sealed divisions. Hamra was far from immune. During the Israeli siege of Beirut and the bombardment of the Palestinian refugee camps in the west, shells fell on Hamra's residential streets and killed civilians. Hamra was considered a war zone: flags of surrender were hung from balconies and roof-tops, Palestinian Fatah guerrillas drove guns into the streets and told civilians to take refuge in their basements, the place stank of faeces after the water supply was cut off and rubbish accumulated on the streets.[6] But it was not only the Israelis who had an impact: the Israel-supported Lebanese Forces of Bachir Gemayel fought Muslim militias. Eventually this Christian coalition broke into factions and so it continued, with the local abduction of foreigners (such as Brian Keenan and John McCarthy) from 1984-1987. Hamra felt sealed off and anti-western feeling developed. Highly significant in the denominational mix was the influx of rural Shia fleeing Israeli aggression in the south and refugees from east Beirut.

Arab novels set during the war can highlight on the one hand the sense of displacement, distaste and fascination felt by working-class rural and refugee families confronted with the westernized freedom of some women in Hamra, its mixed café culture and different ways of speaking (Hassan Daoud, *Sanat al-utumatik* 1996).[7] On the other hand, one protagonist notes how the cosmopolitan Café de Paris had become a male bastion and how the area had lost its elegance and become proletarian: it was now full of militiamen, refugees, prostitutes, street vendors, armed vehicles and rubbish (Sonallah Ibrahim, *Beirut, Beirut,* 1984).[8] Difficult contrasts are inevitable in a city as small as Beirut, and for some Hamra was Paris before it disintegrated, whereas for others, together with the Palestinian camp of Sabra (the targeted site of bombings and massacres) (Mu'nis al Razzaz *Ahyā fi al-bahr al Mayyit*), it was more like Hanoi.[9]

It is impossible to imagine the main street of Hamra as having ever been elegant or sophisticated. The main interest of this street for the foreign visitor is its life and jumble of retail activity. Businessmen, shopkeepers, students, maids, street vendors, foreigners, visitors and all of Hamra's mixed population throng the streets and cafés. Many seek out the not cheap, but by central Beirut standards, reasonably priced clothes and the contents of other shops. Here the shop windows are a delight:

trainers with multi-coloured appliqués; voluminous, encrusted, revealing evening gowns for divas, curvaceous female dummies in black leather body suits, muscled male ones with bronzed plastic bodies showing off sportswear, suits for the gentleman about town and day wear for conservative Muslim ladies. Names such as the Dernier Cri boutique next to a crumbling apartment block speak of past glories and past fashion. Of these relics the Café de Paris survived until 2019 with a custom of mostly respectable looking gentlemen of a certain age reading newspapers. In 2021 it had been replaced by the café/restaurant God Father.

The famous Horseshoe Café has also lost its past identity and is now Rossa, but joining its ghosts of literary and artistic figures is the singer and actress Sabah. She beams out like a planet enclosed in rings of Arabic calligraphy from a mural on the side wall of the building, reminding people, in the words of the artist Yazan Halwani, that there was a non-sectarian era of culture before the civil war. His philosophy is not only to

Some of the delights of Hamra Street (Beatrice Teissier)

represent giant cultural figures as a reminder of the past and as a social bond to combat Lebanon's partisan attitudes, but also to humanize the destitute and to foster a sense of community. The artist acknowledges that he cannot hope to change the country, but aspires to make a contribution.[10]

People today say how down at heel Hamra has become since the economic crisis, and it is true that shops have closed and many vendors sit in the dark, but nothing can erase its life force. 'What can we do?' asked one shopkeeper, 'we keep going for our families, but we feel Lebanon has been abandoned to crooks'. The crowded side streets of Hamra give the impression that, with a minimum of effort, anything can be still found here: there are food and fruit stalls, supermarkets, mechanics, cafés and kebab stalls, hotels, apartment blocks ranging from scruffy to luxurious. Computer and mobile phone buffs sit in tiny shops and will fix anything technical for you. First class hospitals are down the road. There are also half-built constructions, parking lots and mysterious, derelict spaces, and further afield, as on Maamari Street, abandoned period properties.

To the west, before Hamra Street terminates in a fork, is small market selling preserves, jewellery, ostrich eggs and other sundries. This is overlooked by another vast mural, this time from another culture. A snub-nosed, slit-eyed figure shrouded in patterned peasant-like clothes with a string of chillies around the neck, holds a lamb in hands that appear tattooed. Below is a bundle resembling a sandal with a small doll-like figure (these appear in many of his works) and what look like offerings. This work, entitled *Pagano*, is by the Chilean artist Inti, whose name derives from the Quecha word for sun. His work uses vibrant colours referencing Latin America and often features these mysterious snub-nosed creatures with head coverings, who seem to subvert Christian iconography with indigenous and 'peasant' themes from traditional Chilean culture, but also holding or sitting close to universal symbols such as a heart, a skull, bullets, a diamond or more specifically indigenous ones like the miniature figures, maize and chillies. His work is international, and while the witty confessional reference may appeal to some Hamra residents, others may not like it, unless they think of it as a cartoon.

Another market, a Sunday one, is to be found by the Catholic Church of St Francis (off the eastern end of Hamra). On Sunday this church is packed with Filipino maids on their day off. After mass they sit, with Sri Lankan ladies, in the small garden of the church overlooked by the Virgin in a grotto, chatting, bartering, doing their hair and nails. Nearby, the small market, the air redolent with garlic and soy sauce, sells every Filipino delicacy to cater for the homesick, from fried chicken feet to marinated meats and vegetables, as well as clothes, handbags, shoes, toiletries and jewellery.

A down to earth reality which cannot be ignored, and is particularly in evidence in Hamra, is the consequence of a more recent civil war and the recent economic crisis: refugees from Syria. Mothers with their infants and toddlers squat on pavements, often a few metres from each other, begging, while the more aggressive older children dart among cars and into cafés or tug at strangers' sleeves asking for food. Teenage girls hang around the streets or go about in groups of two and threes. Occasionally they get picked up by taxis. Older boys may have a shoe-shining kit or try and sell paper handkerchiefs or, more recently, masks. Sheltered empty spaces are rented by those who can afford them, and there are occasional sightings of *niqab*-clad women on the balconies of half-built, windowless apartment buildings. In 2021 men and youths were chest deep in rubbish bins taking what they could.

These refugees are all despised and mostly ignored by the

*Pagano* by Inti (Beatrice Teissier)

Lebanese and the refrains are consistent: watch out for your things, don't give money to the children, they work in gangs, we have no space for them, and remember what the Syrians did to us during the war. One conspiracy theory current in the street is that the Syrian refugees are being paid to stay in Lebanon, for fear that if they go back home, they will take a boat from Latakia and try to go to Europe. To date Syrian refugee children are the only members of this displaced community, despite the severe economic crisis, who bother anyone. Occasionally elderly or unemployed Lebanese sit quietly on street corners with their hands outstretched.

Walking east on Hamra Street you will pass multiple banks and a derelict-looking building with papers stacked against its windows and from where the occasional neon light flickers. This used to be the Ministry of Tourism, which was partly renovated until vandalized. There will then be a choice to walk north-west to the Sanayeh Gardens or to continue towards Kantari, passing the Haigazian Armenian University, towards Bab Idriss and the centre, or turning into the university and Jumblatt quarter.

1 My thanks to Hayat Gebara for this information.
2 Kassir 2011, 390, notes, without a reference, that the name may be derived from a Persian community, the Hamra, who supposedly passed through the area. In Persian the word means 'companion, fellow traveller, part of a retinue'. How this might be applied to Beiruti Hamra is not clear. My thanks to John Gurney for this information.
3 Khalaf 1973, 112-113.
4 Kassir 2011, 417.
5 Hayek 2015, 67; Kassir 1994, 135.
6 Fisk 2001, 230, 293.
7 Aghacy 2015, 94, from Hassan Daoud *Sanat-al-utumatik* 1996.
8 ibid 83-84, from Sonallah Ibrahim, *Bayrūt-Bayrūt,* Beirut: Dār al-Mustaqbal al-'Arabi.
9 ibid 11, from Mu'nis al Razzaz *Ahyā fi al-bahr al-mayyit,* Beirut: al-Mu'assasa al-'Arabiyya li-l-Dirāsat wā-l-Nashr.
10 Najjar 2015, 30. Other works by this artist in Beirut are to be found off Bliss Street, Gemmayze and Sodeco.

# 3. MISSIONARIES AND RADICALS
# THE AMERICAN UNIVERSITY OF BEIRUT

IT IS DIFFICULT TO IGNORE, walking through the Moorish arch of AUB's main entrance on Bliss Street (having first negotiated with security guards) that you are stepping into a privileged world: this much is evident not only in the steps that take the visitor down to a plaza and the graceful sandstone building of College Hall, but in the tidy recycling bins, the no-smoking instructions (extended to metres outside the entrance) and the well-tended avenues leading to the campus and its vast park. It is also in the entitled swagger of certain students. The sense of relief and pleasure at being away from the fast food and traffic chaos of Bliss Street is undeniable. In the autumn of 2021 access to the campus was limited to staff and students: a combination of factors due to Covid, security and possibly ongoing repairs to damage from the port explosion.

AUB's campus stretches over thirty hectares along Bliss Street down to the sea, and contains over eighty buildings, including a medical centre and teaching hospital (AUBMC) and an multiple sclerosis centre outside the campus.

Founded as the Syrian Protestant College, AUB arose out of the denominational competition between the French, German and Orthodox missions of the mid-nineteenth century. A charter for the College was granted from the State of New York in 1863, with the fundraising participation of its first president, Daniel Bliss (1866-1902). The College first opened with sixteen students in premises in Zokak el Blat,[1] and in 1870 a

The horseshoe arch to the main entrance of AUB on Bliss Street
(Beatrice Teissier)

large tract of land, consisting mostly of Druze-owned mulberry
plantations, was acquired in Ras Beirut. By 1874 College Hall
and the clock tower were complete and became the catalyst that
changed forever the character of Ras Beirut and propelled the
expansion of the city westwards.

The Protestant College was designed along American campus lines, architecturally much in keeping with the trend for sober Gothic revival (with early nods to the Romanesque), which became popular from the mid-1860s in American educational institutions such as Bryn Mawr, Yale and Princeton.[2] Thus the main characteristics of this Gothic style (an imposing gateway, crenellation, a clock tower, a chapel with rosette window, pointed arches and trefoils) are features of the early American Halls and other buildings of the Protestant College but these were tempered by the use of local features such as sandstone, red-tiled roofs, multiple arches and arabesques in lieu of Gothic tracery and an eccentric reference to Moorish architecture in the design of the solid main gate (by the American architect, Edward Pearce Casey). The late nineteenth- and early twentieth-century buildings and 'Halls' (Post, Sage, College, Ada Dodge, Daniel Bliss) of the campus show none of the extravagance of *fin-de-siècle* Beirut architecture elsewhere: they attempt to personify the spirit of collegiate sobriety prevalent in the early days of the College, but they remain (except for the rebuilt College Hall, see below), one of the few remaining authentic and harmonious architectural complexes from that period. They fortunately still stand their own among the onslaught of most modern developments of the campus, including the brutal concrete distortion that is the Issam Fares Institute for Public Policy (Zaha Hadid architects, 2014) which cuts a swathe of disharmony in an otherwise beautiful space. This building, like much of modern Beirut's architecture, is testimony to the indiscriminate worship of 'famous' architects and anything they might create without regard to context (see Appendix).

The College's mission, as asserted by Daniel Bliss in 1871, was open to 'all conditions and classes of men, without regard to colour, nationality, race or religion' on the understanding that the teachings of Rome and the East

A jarring sight, the Issam Fares Building on AUB campus
(Beatrice Teissier)

were superstitious and erroneous and that the only path to salvation and truth was through Presbyterianism. As further asserted by the Rev George Post in a public lecture in London in 1888, College Hall was a 'lighthouse' standing in order to enlighten the Mahommedan world and bring it to the cross.[3] Prayer attendance was mandatory for all. This non-liberal, paternalistic attitude had consequences. Edwin Lewis, the Professor of Chemistry, Physics and Geology, was dismissed, in a campaign led by George Post, for speaking favourably about Charles Darwin at the college graduation ceremony of 1882. This resulted in student and staff protests and the resignation of Cornelius van Dyck, the Professor of Pathology, who was also an Arabist and astronomer. Students were suspended. In changing times and post-World War I, a more secular approach was favoured, partly because the mixed denominational intake necessitated a mitigation of sectarian differences. The College's programmes were expanded and it was renamed as the American University of Beirut in 1921.[4] The University's educational reputation quickly gained prestige: not only for its teaching of sciences and languages (Bible studies included at first), but also for the teaching and practice of its medical departments) for which AUB was to become renowned.[5] Female students were admitted in 1927.[6]

Teaching was at first in Arabic, but by 1880, it turned to English, despite local objections. Today the students are impressively fluent in written and spoken English, although the everyday Arabo-English chatter is infused with American slang (since school) that is the despair of some parents who believe their offspring are forgetting how to speak proper Arabic.

Despite, or perhaps because of, its strict Presbyterian beginnings and its educational ambitions, AUB became (and has remained) a hub for political activism at all levels, from international communism and socialism to student-led campus revolts. It has been said that AUB has at times been a microcosm for Middle Eastern politics (such as Arab nationalism, the Palestinian question, even Zionism until 1948) to be played out.[7] For example, the Beirut Reform Society, which advocated decentralization and representative politics and whose founding members included Salim Salam (an enlightened Beiruti public figure, eventually President of the Municipality of Beirut and opponent of the French Mandate), and Ahmad Mukhtar Bayhum (Mayor of Beirut) defied the authorities and met at the College in 1913 approving a general strike in protest at the hard line of the status quo. A delegation of the Reform movement went to Paris for the Arab Congress of 1913, whose goal was to discuss reforms and autonomy in the Ottoman Empire.[8] In the event World War I intervened and the disintegration of the Ottoman Empire ensued. The College also had to navigate outside forces: in 1917 Jamal Pasha (the repressive Governor of Greater Syria under the Ottomans) declared the College an Ottoman College and himself a patron; in 1918 the College fêted General Allenby, and at the Paris Peace Conference of 1919 Bliss, as a regional adviser, promoted regional autonomy, and the right to chose which power should be in charge.[9] This was a utopian vision, as in consequence of the 1916 Sykes-Picot agreement, the French gained the mandate for Greater Syria.

The University witnessed particularly strong student Palestinian movements. In the 1960s and 1970s there were brawls between left-wing Palestinian supporters and conservative elements. There was also a student strike at the time over tuition fees, which descended into violence and damage to the campus.[10] The University was far from immune to the civil war: lectures and campus life continued as much as they could but were interrupted and standards fell as the area turned increasingly violent. At first the University was granted neutral status, and its security entrusted to a Palestinian group, but after the Israeli invasion of 1982, other militias (Druze, Shia, later Syrian) took control of west Beirut and anti-western, notably anti-American, feeling prevailed. The period 1982-86 was marked by a series of assassinations – University President Malcom Kerr, 1984, Peter Kilburn, a University librarian, 1984, the English instructor Denis Hill, 1985 - and abductions: President Dodge, 1982, Professor Frank Regier, 1984, the Dean of Agriculture, Thomas Sutherland, 1985, David Jacobsen, Director of the American University Hospital, 1985, Professor Nabil Matar, 1986, Brian Keenan and John McCarthy, 1986, mostly western but also Lebanese members of staff. A suicide bomber killed and injured people at the University Hospital in 1987, and shelling became more extreme during the last phase of the war (1989). A bomb virtually destroyed (the now rebuilt) College Hall in 1991.[11]

AUB has, perhaps inevitably, been variously accused of elitism, Arab nationalism and being an agent of the CIA.[12] Only insiders know whether there is any truth to the more recent assertion (by a member of staff, Steven Salanita, a vociferous critic of Israel who was denied tenure) that freedom of political activism and debate has been curtailed, and that the University seeks to impose a corporate and American-leaning foreign policy.[13] Certainly the budget is sponsored mostly from the US and it has been known for academics from other higher educational establishments in Beirut to confide darkly, 'I would never go to the Americans (to teach).' The University's local outreach programmes certainly smack of soft power. Be that as it may, having a degree from AUB means something not only in Lebanon but internationally, and students continue to be vocal in a campus where religious identities, despite anti-confessional movements, cannot be separated from their culture and where the world around them is unstable. The novel *Beirut 2002* by Renée Hayek portrays post-civil war AUB students as pleasure seeking, living in the moment, ignoring the past and distracting themselves from underlying anxieties about their future with drink and drugs.[14] It would, of course, be equally plausible to write about a group of students or an individual, who witnessing corruption, sectarianism, damage to the environment or heritage and exorbitant fees in the wake of the economic crisis, become active in the best interests of their country or militant. Endless variations are possible. At first glance, the relaxed demeanour of the undergraduates does fit a picture of young, nonchalant and moneyed privilege, but also masks ambition, anger and more often than not the desire to get out of the country.

The grounds of AUB are a delight. Despite the encroaching buildings, it is the trees and other vegetation and sea views that are the enchantment of this place and would gratify any botanist or arborist. Strolling through the campus with its giant Italian cypresses (including one planted by Daniel Bliss), fig, olive and orange trees, different palms, a superb Banyan, coral trees, laurel trees, hibiscus, jasmine, wild cyclamen and roses, or sitting on a bench (in the company of cats) while overlooking the sea and away from city clamour, is one of the greatest privileges of this institution. Visitors with scientific minds might also want to see the Natural History Museum (of plants and animals from the region) whose collections were started by Drs Post and van Dyck from the 1850s to the 1870s and learn about the Post Herbarium, which holds each of the plant species described in Post's *Flora of Syria, Palestine and Sinai* (1883, 1896 ), published by the Protestant College. This work has since been revised several times, and the collection continuously updated (although field work was interrupted during the civil war) and re-curated. The Geology Museum was created in the same spirit of research in 1958.

Another collection which has great significance for the region is the Archaeological Museum. It was founded with a donation of Cypriot pottery from the amateur archaeologist and American Consul in Larnaca, Luigi Palma di Cesnola, in 1868, and originally curated by George Post in a room in College Hall, before it was moved to its present location, Post Hall, completed in 1902. This museum is modern and well designed, and its collections are chronologically arranged, from the Palaeolithic to the Islamic periods. It provides a good introduction (or reminder if one has already visited the National Museum) of not only the richness of the area's archaeology but the variety of its early foreign contacts, which give context to the origins of urban Beirut. The museum shows none of the dismissive approach to archaeology witnessed in Beirut city centre, but unfortunately did not escape the effects of the port explosion, when a whole case of Roman glass was blown to smithereens. Public access to these museums, with the exception of the Archaeological Museum, is dependent on local circumstances and is not guaranteed.

1  Hanssen 2005a, 183.
2  Goodchild 2000, 279-282.
3  Hanssen 2005a, 183.
4  http://www.aub.edu.lb.ulibraries/Pages
5  Kassir 2011, 179ff.
6  ibid, 319.
7  Oweini 1996, 4; Kahlenberg 2019.
8  Kassir 2011, 240-243.
9  http://www.aub.edu.lb.ulibraries/Pages/index.aspx
10 Oweini 1996, 4.
11 ibid, 8.
12 ibid, 4.
13 mondoweiss.net/2017/08aub-limited
14 Aghacy 2015, 187-188.

# 4. FROM GOTHIC TO HIGH-RISE BLISS STREET

IF PRESIDENT BLISS WERE TODAY to step out from the AUB's main gate into the street named after him he would not find the dirt road of old, but be faced with the bright yellow arches of the McDonald's logo directly across the road. Someone might explain to him that this is the symbol of one of America's cherished exports (or an example of food colonialism responsible for the obesity of millions). He would find a street engulfed in a rush of activity: familiar sandstone buildings with pitched roofs and lunettes taken over by fast food outlets, juice bars, mobile phone vendors and small supermarkets, as well as smart cafés interspersed with dreary concrete blocks.

Students come and go, negotiate the stream of traffic, smoke (outside the perimeter area), drink coffee, greet each other with a *merhaba* (hello), 'how goes it man?' *kif ik/ak?* (how are you f/m?), the occasional *ça va?*, all in 2021 peppered with the word 'visa'. The street is busy with cars, motorbikes and people even early in the morning: businessmen and women consult their computers or have meetings in cafés while chairs are still being put out, staff from the University or hospitals and students rush in for a take away coffee or pastry, or stand outside the small coffee booth by the second entry to the University (closer to the Van Dyck stairs) and chat around the giant banyan tree as cats roam looking out for the food put out for them. On the pavement opposite the main entrance a refugee boy might already be squatting trying to sell one or two packets of tissues, or offering to clean your shoes with minimal equipment, and further down the road a Syrian woman with a baby will already be setting herself up for the day as her two older children dart among cars, tug at strangers or try to infiltrate cafés, begging.

Walking west towards what is technically Ras Beirut (or the tip of Beirut, although the whole area including Hamra is known as such) the street offers a multitude of varied and disjointed sights characteristic of Beirut: from historic monuments to alien looking high-rises, with oddities in between. Leaving the agitation around AUB, the small Ottoman (but painted and renovated) Daouk Mosque is a reminder of the historic position of this family in this area of Beirut. The Daouks settled in Beirut from Morocco in the fifteenth century and became one of the city's patrician families, closely associated with the Sinno and Ardati families. Its members include Omar Daouk (1875-1949), politician, businessman, philanthropist and President of the Chamber of Commerce, who helped draft the Lebanese constitution,[1] and Ahmad Daouk (1892-1979), businessman, politician, Prime Minister of Lebanon (1941, 1960).[2] Both have streets named after them, and there is a square named after Omar Daouk with a bust of him by the Armenian sculptor Mkrtich Mazmanian in the centre. They family now owns a spectacular villa in Clemenceau, and another in Sursock.

The visitor will pass colourfully painted houses and on the opposite side of the road, the street's own ruined folly (still there in 2021): a roofless, Chinoiserie-themed restaurant and market (now housing a snack bar on the ground floor), with volute lintels above shuttered windows and a dilapidated balcony, all with Art Deco railings. Balanced precariously on the edge of the concrete roof ledge, and above the outline of a Chinoiserie structure are the remains of the original sign - 'Mini Chinese' - now reduced to 'hines' with a sun symbol behind it, and below, in different lettering and profiting from the ready-made round symbol, 'Pizza Papa.'

Dilapidated Bliss Street Chinoiserie (Beatrice Teissier)

Continuing west you may encounter 'hedgehog' metal defences or razor wire on the road and a checkpoint. Behind a militarized concrete barricade on the right stands the modern, imposing Embassy of Saudi Arabia, its isolation and security symbolizing the volatile relations between the kingdom and Lebanon. Saudi Arabia has historically propped up Lebanon in times of trouble, but this has now stopped in the wake of Hezbollah's ascendancy. Relations were at a particular low in the autumn of 2021 when Saudi Arabia was criticized by a Lebanese politician for its involvement in Yemen. The building is built in a neo-Mamluk style, reminiscent of the Municipality Building in the centre but with a block of projecting wooden latticed windows traditional of Arabic domestic architecture (*mashrabiya*). On the left beleaguered apartment blocks from the 1920-1940s stand between and opposite high-rises of various degrees of height, taste and extravagance. One early period block stands out in particular for it shows the superimposition of different styles of balcony and windows over seven floors: from a square first-floor verandah and one floor with a rounded balcony and rounded pillars to two plain rounded balconies and one that in 2019 was festooned with densely packed small toys (looking rather like an invasion of multiplying microbes) and a balcony consisting of bay windows replacing the traditional tripartite recessed doors and windows. This optimization of space over time is found in numerous surviving apartment blocks of this period as is the individualization of verandahs or balconies, whether with plants or art.

This area used to be a hub of such homes, but the march of destruction and reconstruction has advanced steadily in what is a prime location. A businessman returning to the area after five years away was horrified to find that a 'beautiful old villa' on the right side of the road had been replaced by a monstrous, gated high rise with all amenities. For the rich here, however, this new kind of living seems *de rigueur*. An apartment with a decent sea view (from US$1.5-2.5 million upwards) might give you open-plan spaces, multiple bedrooms, several bathrooms, a 'space for the maid', large, shaded balconies with loungers and play area for children, electric shutters, secure parking, a roof garden, gym and/or swimming pool and round-the-clock security, generators, state-of-the-art lifts and a small decorative green space outside - and a monitored secure gate. Many of these flats are investments, however, and lie empty for much of the year. Those used to the traditional space of a house or apartment might ask what it might mean to live so cocooned, surrounded by like-minded people in a kind of luxurious uniformity. This is the appeal of the wealthy tower block ghettos, however; the city is viewed as chaotic and mostly unclean, requiring a chauffeur on standby, and is never to be walked in (maids do all the shopping). For the ordinary people of Beirut, many living in concrete boxes with canvas draped over balconies, this is another world, even universe.

A narrow road on the right, in the midst of a leafy, human-scale residential area, will bring you to the Manara: the site of the old Ottoman lighthouse (1825). The present, black and white striped lighthouse was built between 1953 and 1957, replacing a 1920s predecessor, which in turn was originally built adjacent to the Ottoman original, until both were demolished. Like so many of Beirut's monuments this lighthouse did not escape the civil war: it was turned off during the Israeli invasion of 1982, but still bombarded and its keeper kidnapped. It was again targeted in 2006, with the keepers inside. Nor did it avoid the surge of development when the eighteen-storey Manara 587, which, breaking regulations and despite objections, was approved, blocking a view of the lighthouse from the front. The lighthouse is now guarded by the military, and a new, unobstructed lighthouse by the Corniche was built in 2003, with funds contributed by the developer of the skyscraper.[3]

To the right of the Manara is another historic monument: the Maison Rose, a residential villa built by a member of another of Beirut's patrician families, Mohammed Ardati, in the early 1880s, on top of an old hunting lodge. The house, whose stunning double terrace is visible from the Corniche, is now in bad state of disrepair, but some of its essential features can be seen from the back. From this side the house is on two floors, with arched canopies over

A view of the Old Manara and the Maison Rose from the Corniche
(Beatrice Teissier)

the entrances and with a side staircase with cast-iron railings. The upper floor has two doors with triangular lunettes above and rectangular windows to the side. The ground floor has a door with a horseshoe arch and a row of arched windows (now boarded up from the inside). Most of the glass in all the windows is broken, but apparently the coloured glass that characterizes some of these period houses is still visible inside the house's central hall. It has a split-level garden and will still have at least a partially magnificent view of the sea beyond the development on the hill beneath it. The Maison Rose has been inhabited by several owners: the Daouks first shared it with the Ardatis, it was then leased to a number of individuals and their families, and subsequently occupied by the Khazem family until 2014, when it was also used as a venue for art exhibitions and other cultural events. It was then sold to a property developer (Hisham Jaroudi), who promised to have it renovated. It seems that there are ongoing problems with this process.[4]

Leaving this area, Bliss Street splits into two, Bliss loops downhill past the German International School, while Najib Ardati Street curves down to meet Bliss again at the forlorn looking (from this side anyway) Al Nadi Al Riyadi (predominantly basketball) sports club. This club, founded in the 1930s, is associated with the Sunni 'Future Movement'. Najib Ardati Street features briefly in Annia Ciezadlo's memoir *A Memoir of Food, Love and War* (2011) as being very close to sites of confrontation between Sunni and Shia gangs in 2007, each wanting to claim the area as their own. Today all is quiet. Beyond is the hellish double-lane freeway (Charles de Gaulle) and the Corniche, facing the Military Beach.

1    https:www.archivelebanon.com/dax-omar-muhammad-bey-daouk
2    https:www.archivelebanon.com/dax-ahmad-muhammad-bey-daouk
3    Karen Karam 2016.
4    Fisk 2016; 2017 http:/www.levantineheritage.com/lost-houses-beirut.
     html

# 5. OTTOMANS, ARMENIANS AND DRUZE SANAYEH TO JUMBLATT

CONTINUING EASTWARDS ON HAMRA STREET, there are several choices: walk north-west towards the Sanayeh or René Moawad Gardens, continue west towards Kantari, passing the Haigazian Armenian University and on to Bab Idriss and the centre, or to turn into Mexico Street past the University to the Jumblatt quarter.

Whichever direction is chosen you will not escape from the part of the street known on some maps as 'Bank of Lebanon'. Banks, private and commercial, owned by a cabal of powerful families and individuals, are everywhere in Beirut. The state and banking sector are interdependent in Beirut, and it is the banks that traditionally held the country stable, whereas now they are considered, together with successive governments, as having brought the country to its knees.

Beirut has had an active banking sector since the nineteenth century, and during the 1960s and early 1970s, the city became the financial centre of the Arab world and a base for investment: banks attracted oil money and remittances from those escaping centralized Arab economies and because of secure reserves and its secrecy laws. The Lebanese pound has traditionally been pegged to the US dollar since the 1990s and this, with dollar reserves, kept the currency stable while offering extremely high interest rates for deposits (essential to the Lebanese consumer, paid in Lebanese pounds). High yielding bonds also helped pay off the national debt. Since the civil war there has been and still is competition from Dubai, but the sector was known for its resilience and managed to profit from the financial crisis of 2008 by attracting cash.

Banking was not immune from shocks, however; the war in Syria slowed down remittances and money from the Gulf and civil disturbances in the autumn of 2019 (first over a tax hike, and then in massive protests against the country's political elite for corruption, poor infrastructure and unemployment) flagged up the difficulties of the banking sector and led to uncertainty and crisis. There were fears that Lebanon would be unable to pay off its huge (over 150 per cent of GDP) debt and would default on the extremely high yielding Eurobonds which had been issued. The crisis was made clear on the streets when banks were closed for several weeks and controls were imposed on local dollar withdrawals (leading to a black market in dollars) and money sent abroad. The Lebanese pound/lira was devalued and the dollar peg changed from 1.500 to 1.900. The anchor for the Lebanese pound was from now on lost. This had an immediate impact on local businesses; salaries were unpaid, shops empty, shopkeepers threatened with bankruptcy, others could not pay their rents. Prime Minister, Rafik Hariri, stepped down in October 2019.

Experts agree that Lebanon's economy is in a terrible shape due to mismanagement, corruption and debt, and that reforms are needed. In the event, Lebanon did manage to pay off its Eurobond debt of some US2 billion in time (November 2019) and was promised help from the Arab League and the US, and from Europe only on condition of serious reforms. One such measure entailed an audit of the Banque du Liban and others, whose dealings remain profoundly opaque. Since then the situation has become far worse: by June of 2020 the Lebanese pound had lost 80 per cent of its value and continued to fall, as did foreign currency reserves. Then the explosion happened and by the summer of 2021, amidst revolving door prime ministers, there was still no government (one was eventually formed in early September, with the tycoon Najib Mikati as PM (see p. 143).

A cash economy (in dollars when possible) became the norm in an environment of soaring prices (annual inflation at 85 per cent by 2021) and with it civil unrest, electricity cuts, shortages of everything from medicine to fuel and even bread. The black market thrived as did the sale of subsidized goods to Syria. Hezbollah stepped in with organized relief (ration cards, food, fuel), some coming from Iran and thus further panicking the US about the stability of the region. Help from other quarters was still promised on condition of reforms. The World Bank concentrated efforts on a project aimed at Lebanon's poorest 200,000, but this was also delayed due to monitoring problems and how recipient families should be selected. With the state failing to help, food banks were organized by ordinary citizens. A further aid conference was organized for August 2021. By this time the situation for most salaried Lebanese or those who had not managed to get their money out of the country was dire. Salaries had lost most of the value, bank deposits were seized with only minimal sums allowed to be withdrawn in local currency only and at a far lower rate than the real black-market rate (fluctuating at around LP 20,000-22,000 to US$1). People were losing their savings.

Those working abroad or dealing with foreigners could still be paid in what is now termed 'fresh' dollars. Dollars can be exchanged at a decent rate in money exchange booths, many of which sprang up in Hamra. Some money exchangers come to people's homes, where dollars are hidden, carrying millions of worthless Lebanese pounds in black plastic bags. The banks are effectively bankrupt, the result of corruption and a policy that people say was no more than a grotesque Banque du Liban Ponzi scheme. In October 2021 the IMF was said to have started official contacts with the government. In November, Mikati stated that the 'talks were going well'. But people have their opinion of the IMF as well: 'International Mother Fuckers' announced one example of graffiti.

## Spears and Sanayeh

If choosing to go towards Sanayeh Gardens you will have to cross Spears street.[1] A stroll along this street reveals a variety of 1920-1940s apartment blocks distinguished by different curved, rectangular or other geometrically shaped window doors and windows, glass fretwork, elaborate cast-iron balconies and pillars with different capitals. One such building can be seen at the intersection of Fakhreddine and Spears.[2] Spears Street also contains some very damaged villas that seem to be waiting in limbo. One in particular (between Spears, Michel Chiha and May Ziade) is typical of the late nineteenth-century wealthy merchants' mansions. Built around 1880 by Hassan Naamani (a textile importer, with additional businesses in Iraq and Manchester), the red-tiled mansion (best seen from a bird's eye view) is double storeyed and has the traditional three arched (pointed and curved) central widows and doors, some with decorated glass, as well as trefoil oculi and western-style rectangular windows. The entrance off Michel Chiha Street previously had a double, marble clad semi-circular staircase (now semi-ruined) and led to a park with a circular pool and fountain. A colonnaded portico with a terrace was to the west. The two main floors had apartments and utilities arranged around a central hall (with a hexagonal southern end). As with many of these houses, there were multiple owners and lodgers. The house was bought in 1931 by Mohammed Abboud Abdel el Merhabi, whose widow then married a future Prime Minister of Lebanon, Takieddine el Solh (1973-74). The ground floor was partially rented to the Ammoun family from 1919 to 1973. It was then besieged by squatters. By 2005 the mansion was set for demolition, but it has won a reprieve, although litigation between the heirs is ongoing.[3] Older and other such mansions with similar fates are found in Zokak el Blat.

The Sanayeh Gardens and adjoining buildings are late Ottoman period relics that are fortunately in good shape. Here you will see examples of city developments made under Sultan Abdul Hamid II (1842-1918) during this time. Public works and infrastructure came to Beirut after it was made a provincial capital in 1888 (previously it had been annexed to Damascus). Together with modernizations such as the extension to the harbour, the building of the Petit Serail and the Manara lighthouse, two other significant public buildings were established here: the Sanayeh Arts and Crafts building, an adjacent hospital and the gardens opposite. The plain, two-storey sandstone buildings were sited on what was the windblown plateau of Ramlat al Zarif and greatly contributed to the expansion and status of the city outside its cramped centre. The school was to teach manufacturing and arts and crafts to underprivileged students and potential merchants, entrepreneurs or industrialists.[4] The Arts and Crafts building was inaugurated in 1907 and a photograph of the time shows the then Wali (governor general) of Beirut (Khalil Pasha), rows of dignitaries, a military guard, soldiers, a military band and in the distance escorted ladies with parasols standing in a bare space in front of the building.[5] The renovated buildings now form part of the heavily guarded Ministry of the Interior, with an area supposedly kept for the Lebanese National Library.

By 1925 the garden was fully developed along symmetrical lines, with a central pool, benches, avenues and carefully planted flower beds. Much of its layout was as it is today, but with fewer trees. A feature of the garden is the white marble fountain dedicated to Sultan Abdul Hamid II to mark the twenty-fifth year of his accession to the throne (he ruled from 1876 and was deposed in 1909). The grandiosity and calligraphy of the Hamidiye fountain which included the Sultan's large gold leafed monogram (*tughra*), was aimed at fostering a personality cult.[6] The fountain, sculpted by Yusuf al-Anid, is also an example of the originality of its architect-engineer designer, Yussuf Aftimus (1866-1952). Aftimus' main legacy is in the centre of the city; his work is characterized by an eclectic style with Moorish, Islamic, Ottoman, vernacular and personal elements. In the fountain's case, the style is neo-Ottoman or Islamic pastiche. Like much of Beirut's heritage, the fountain's presence in the garden is the result of displacement. The fountain was originally situated in what is now Riad al Solh (originally Assour) Square: a photograph of 1903 shows its original placement at the junction of two roads leading from Zokak el Blat and Bachoura. The Grand Serail was behind it.[7] The inauguration of the fountain (c.1900) was a grand affair, with a symbolic drink taken from it by the Wali, witnessed by the notables of the town and the public.[8] The fountain was moved to the garden in 1957 to make place for a statue of Riad al Solh.

Today the garden is officially known as the René Moawad Gardens, after the thirteenth President of Lebanon, assassinated in 1989 after seventeen days in office while returning from Independence Day celebrations in west Beirut.[9]

The garden did not escape the civil war: during the Israeli assault on west Beirut in 1986, bombs fell on nearby buildings which housed mostly squatters from the refugee camps of Sabra and Chatila who had taken refuge in the garden. Fisk describes bloodied women shrieking among the trees.[10] In a subsequent Israeli onslaught (2006) the garden served as a centre for coordinating relief work for internally displaced people who fled Israel's bombardment in the south and the southern suburbs of Beirut. In post-war Arab literature the garden exemplifies the degradation during the civil war: a drunk lurches in the garden holding on to his trousers[11] and the depleted central pool is used as a washing and swimming facility by children during the attacks of 2006.[12] After years of neglect the garden was re-opened in 2014 with the aid of the NGO Azadea Foundation.

Today the garden is clean and sedate and feels reserved. There is a code of conduct panel at the entrance ('no firearms, no alcohol, no smoking, no pets, no motor vehicles,' etc.), which explains its pristine condition. Rules are observed and one feels that exuberance might be frowned upon, despite the children's play area. But the garden is restful: surrounded on three sides by quiet roads, bird song can be heard despite ubiquitous drilling noise in the background. A few refugee stragglers and single males sit on park benches around the large central pool (unfortunately empty in 2021) as do a few elderly couples and conservative Muslim ladies with their babies and

The central pool of Sanayeh Gardens surrounded by a corolla of trees
(Beatrice Teissier)

children. Young men might be seen running round a track. The garden hosts art exhibitions, and life and atmosphere here no doubt changes at different times of the day and on different days of the week, and in different economic circumstances. As with so much of Beirut, this place is given soul by its many beautiful trees  such as Wattle, Coral trees, Eucalyptus Blue Jacaranda and Sago Palms.

Directly opposite the modern entrance (on Alameddine) to the gardens is an old mansion well hidden by trees. To the north-west is the pretty Anis Tabbara Mosque built in traditional style. To the east of Sanayeh, between Medhar Pacha and Buthour, is an apartment block which brings together older traditional architecture (gabled roof, tripartite arched windows, oculi, a roof-top summer room) with later elements such as rectangular windows and wrought-iron balconies.[13] The block looks like two buildings joined together but is not.

## Druze cemetery

Rather than returning north, the curious may want to go south-west and investigate one of the many fascinating cemeteries of Beirut, dotted like a broken mosaic across the city. The Druze cemetery (Tallet ed Druze) occupies a large swathe of land southwards between Roma and Bani Mararouf. Reaching the cemetery via smaller roads in order to avoid the traffic brings the visitor to a partly working-class Muslim area (evident from avenue and street names, such as Algeria, Independence, Sheikh Mohammed Alaya, etc.). The cemetery itself is guarded and is adjacent to a large police station or security facility, and you may have to seek permission to enter. It is nevertheless worth it as it brings the visitor's attention to the important (about 5 per cent) minority that are the Druze in Lebanon, and who are otherwise not highly visible in Beirut. The Druze (of Arab and

Kurdish origin) have been an important presence in Lebanon, fighting against the Franks, since the Crusader period of the eleventh and twelfth centuries. The Chouf mountains were chosen as their base under the Ma'ans (Druze leaders at the time) in the twelfth century, and were later consolidated in the sixteenth and seventeenth centuries, notably under the Ma'an Emir Fakhr al-Din II (1572-1635). The Druze are officially classified as Muslims and currently proclaim themselves as such (for the politics, see Jumblatt below), although their beliefs and practices do not conform to orthodox Islam as they incorporate elements from other belief systems such as Neo-Platonism, Judaism, Christianity and Zoroastrianism. The faith originated as a sect from a Shia-Ismaili background in eleventh-century Cairo; it is monotheistic and Unitarian, and a central tenet of the religion is a belief in reincarnation. Druze practices are secretive and elitist, however; only initiates are allowed to study their scriptures.

The Druze Cemetery with mausolea (Beatrice Teissier)

The cemetery's memorials display the five-coloured (green, red, yellow, blue, white) Druze star, each colour representing metaphysical concepts relevant to the faith, such as white for immanence or green for universal, higher intelligence. Stairs lead the visitor among beautiful, square sandstone mausolea or marble tombs and headstones surrounded by flowering shrubs. Partially lifted tombs and large empty areas carpeted in grasses and wild flowers show that this wealthy looking cemetery is still very much in use. An overgrown enclosure next to one part of the cemetery gives the Druze unexpected, but invited, neighbours: these are the eighteen graves of nationalist 'martyrs' executed at the orders of Jamal Pasha (the governor of Greater Syria) in 1915-16. Destined to have no graves, the Druze have boasted, 'we were the only ones brave enough to defy Jamal Pasha's order to ditch the corpses.'[14]

Opposite the cemetery you may see another of Beirut's mysterious *terrains vagues*, hidden behind panels depicting an idealized 1940s Beirut painted in a naïve style.

### Haigazian, Jumblatt, Kantari

Returning north from Sanayeh, crossing Justinian brings you to the corner of Mexico Street and the Armenian Haigazian University. But before going down Mexico, you may be interested to know that Yussuf Aftimus' villa used to stand on the site of the present Aresco Centre on Justinian before it was pulled down in 1970. It is shocking that this 1925 house, carefully designed to take into account climatic conditions and modern comforts by an architect who contributed so much to the architecture of Beirut, should no longer exist. A photo shows a villa with a flat roof terrace and a large irregularly shaped and pillared portico-verandah (instead of a balcony) set in a park. The façade was said to be deliberately modern and made to contrast with traditional Beiruti façades.[15]

Turning into Mexico Street offers another world from the bustle of Hamra: quiet and clean, with homely cafés and small groups of students. The University building is instantly recognizable by its superimposed arched and colonnaded galleries and by the rocket launcher in its forecourt. This is a proud reminder of the Lebanese Rocket Society's non-militarized space rocket programme spearheaded by Manoug Manougian and students at Haigazian during the early 1960s. The Cedar IV rocket reached 145 kilometres in altitude, but a series of accidents and fear of its military potential caused the programme to be abandoned in the late 1960s.[16]

The University belongs to the youngest of the three Armenian denominational communities in Lebanon: the Evangelical, the other two being Catholic and Orthodox. The University was named after a renowned educator from Konya (Turkey), Dr Armenag Haigazian, who died in the genocide of the 1920s. It was founded as a college for training pastors and leaders of the community in 1955 in partnership with the Missionary Association of America and partly funded by Dr Haigazian's daughter and son-in-law. It was officially pronounced a university in 1996 and is now a pivotal educational institution, and while the governance is evangelical and pastors are still trained there, the University accepts all denominations and does not proselytize. Teaching is in English.[17] The Armenian Evangelical Church was founded in 1846 in Constantinople by a small group stemming from a Bible group, the Pietistical Union, under the influence of missionaries. The community came to Lebanon in 1922 in the wake of the genocide, and their first permanent church in Beirut was founded in 1949 (on Mexico, close to the main University building). The Evangelical community once constituted some 5 per cent of the Armenian population in Lebanon, but since the civil war there has been a steady decline in church attendance, partly due to emigration,

'Arabization' and, it is argued, the Evangelicals' closeness to the Armenian Orthodox community (attending each other's church services or converting).[18] On the question of 'Arabization', the response on the street is a shrug and the observation that 'Armenians have to adapt to where they live' (as is the case with the New Born Christian Armenians in California).

The district is worth wandering around in to find neo-Gothic and other period buildings (May Ziade Street and beyond). The end of Mexico Street is again a different zone: the small cafés are gone, there are checkpoints, and the area feels official, exclusive and high-end residential. High-rises here do not have sun bleached drapes over their balconies. The tone is set by a handsome coloured brick building with a composite façade of rounded bay windows, triple window doors behind small balconies and outer mouldings. The building has an obvious later addition at the top level and modern wings. Luxury is also signalled by well maintained and pretty planting at the entrance. This is the private Trad Hospital, founded in the 1940s, after Dr Fouad Trad, as a maternity hospital.

To the left of the hospital, on the corner of Justinian and America, is the Dar El-Nimer Centre for Arts and Culture, possibly the most attractive and rewarding of Beirut's art centres. This airy white building used to be the private Villa Salem, and was built by Lucien Cavro (1905-78) an architect who worked in Lebanon during the French Mandate (see also the Robert Moawad Museum, p. 196) in the 1930s. The minimalist building circumvented with plain terraces, a tower and with port hole openings to the side was influenced by Le Corbusier, but is lighter in feel. The rows of diamond shapes on the upper part of the rectangular windows, which let in patterns of light and shade, refer to both Arab and late Ottoman/early twentieth-century decorated window traditions, as do the oculi to traditional Beirut nineteenth-century palace architecture.

The open floor plan of the centre hosts exhibitions curated from the private collection of the founder: the Palestinian Rami el Nimer. The collection, made over forty years, is rooted in Palestine and the region and covers centuries of civilization linked to the Islamic world, from ancient manuscripts to icons, from coins to textiles, from arms and armour to postcards, photographs and antiquities. Exhibitions are consequently very wide ranging, but also thematic, and range from Arabic calligraphy to film posters, from modern art installations to photography. The centre also hosts events such as film screenings, workshops, book launches, concerts, story-telling evenings and discussions. Its website (www.darelnimer.org/en/) shows the extraordinary variety of events on offer, some from the diaspora some very local. As part of an Art Film Festival in 2018, there were films such as *May Ziade: Life of an Arab Feminist Writer* (by Mohsen Abd El-Ghani) and on street art in Beirut, *Graffiti Men Beyrouth* (by Sarah Claux). In the autumn of 2019 an exhibition of icons from Jerusalem was postponed because of the widespread demonstrations in Beirut. By the autumn of 2021 museum activity was picking up again after post-explosion renovation work: in October there was a hard-hitting exhibition of contemporary cartoons from all over the Arab world, showing how radical the benign satire and black humour of past years has turned.

Down Justinian from Dar-El Nimer (in the direction of Clemenceau) is the commercial Saleh Barakat gallery, which does not have the intimacy of Dar El-Nimer but which specializes in contemporary art from Lebanon and the rest of the Arab world. In autumn 2021 it hosted an exhibition called *The Show Must Go On*, with monumental canvasses and sculptures expressing what Beirut has endured and is enduring. This was symbolized in one work by a vast tidal wave made of barbed wire (by de Katanani).

## Jumblatt

The area to the left of Mexico is called Jumblatt or Junblatt, after one of the two leading Druze families in Lebanon (the other being Arslan), who have properties in the area. An inaccessible Jumblatt villa in a park (dating from 1897 and once known as Beit Ladki) is off Rebeiz.[19]

The Druze have a strong sense of their role in Lebanon's history and consider their Emirs the 'first founders' (notably Fakhr al-Din II). This is in opposition to Maronite claims on the identity of Lebanon, and there is a history of slaughter between the two communities, most notably in 1860 and against the Phalange in the civil war of 1975-90.

Walid Jumblatt (b. 1949) is currently the most prominent leader of the Druze and leader of the Progressive Socialist Party. His father, Kamal (1917-77) was a major secular, left-wing figure in Lebanese politics who consistently argued for the elimination of the confessional system of politics. He founded the Progressive Socialist Party in 1949 and the Popular Socialist Front in 1953, and while Interior Minister in 1970 legalized the Baath Party[20] and the Lebanese Communist Party. He was awarded the Lenin Prize in 1972.[21] For a minority the Druze have had a significant voice in Lebanese politics: they are known for their canny network of alliances and have had to be pragmatic. This has led to complex and sometimes contradictory relations with other communities and neighbouring countries. For example, Kamal Jumblatt adopted the cause of Nasserite Arabism and was an advocate of the PLO for his own advantage. During the civil war he led a coalition of left-wing parties, but held President Assad of Syria in contempt, which seems to have led to his assassination in 1977. His son Walid succeeded him immediately. The Druze did not resist the Israeli occupation, but Jumblatt subsequently supported demands for an Israeli withdrawal. There was an alliance with the Shia Amal Movement in the 1980s, but a rift after the rise of Hezbollah (formed in 1985). Today Druze policies are more attuned to the politics of confessionalism, but with ongoing tensions with Hezbollah.

## Kantari

To the east of Jumblatt is a district called Kantari, an area of high-end tower blocks, holiday suites and the occasional historic house. The old 'Presidential Palace' or Qasr Hanna Heneine,[22] at the crossing of Kantari/Michel Chiha and Abdel Kader, is an example of the older, late nineteenth-century palaces of Beirut. Built in 1860 (with a second storey in 1870) it has a gabled, red-tiled roof, a sweeping double staircase leading up to a central tripartite arched entrance, oculi and rectangular windows to the side and back. The house was rented multiple times from Hneine's time until Bechara al Khoury (the anti-colonialist, first post-Independence President 1943-52, but also Prime Minister 1927-28, 1929) moved in in 1939. The palace seems to have become a radical centre of resistance against the French. After the resignation of Khoury in 1952, Camille Chamoun, his successor, rented it. Some of the Khoury family moved back in after Chamoun left (1958) and stayed until the area became a civil war hot-spot, when it was occupied by militias. The Khoury family moved back in during the 1980s, before selling it to the Hariri family, who had the palace restored, with a view to turning it into offices for the Hariri Future Movement Party.[23] In the early 2000s it became the offices of Future TV.[24]

While in the area you may be tempted to walk further, cross Clemenceau and join Omar Daouk Street to seek out the restored Omar Daouk residence: an opulent three-floor, turreted mansion built in 1920. Coloured glass can be seen in the upper segments of the windows, star like geometric mouldings on the outer walls and (for those who have access) Arab blessings on the entry wall, ceilings with mouldings, stained glass doors and coloured floor tiles.[25] An adjacent building in a similar style was demolished and replaced by a tower block.

Kantari Street was also the last home in the West of the notorious British spy, Kim Philby. Philby was officially cleared of treason by Prime Minister Harold Macmillan in 1956 although suspicions about him remained.[26] Despite this, Philby came to Beirut as an agent for MI6 under the cover of reporting for the *Observer* and *Economist*. In an atmosphere of Arab nationalism and Cold War conflict, Beirut at the time was a volatile place. In Philby's own words, the city was 'one of the liveliest centres of contraband and espionage in the world'.[27] He had been contacted by the KGB soon after his arrival. The bar of the St George Hotel on the Corniche (see p. 103) was one of the hubs of this world: diplomats, politicians, journalists, spies and academics of all nationalities congregated there, picking up information and gossip while drinking. All spies spied on each other. Beirut was also a heady world of pleasure, with parties, nightlife, beach life and always someone interesting to talk to or to watch. After his third marriage to Eleanor Brewer, Philby moved to a fifth-floor flat in Kantari, and, according to his wife, these were the 'happiest times'.[28] Philby was doing little journalism, but travelling extensively in the region and reporting to the head of British Intelligence in Beirut at the time (Nicholas Elliott) while continuing his double life.[29] He had also turned into a hard drinker. The discovery that George Blake, working for MI6, was a Soviet spy (previously unbeknownst to Philby) triggered warning bells in Philby's mind not felt since the defection of Guy Burgess and Donald Maclean and made him turn to drink even more. This drew attention to him. But the main event which set the scene for his exposure was the testimony of an ardent Zionist, who asserted to the influential Lord Rothschild that Philby had once told her that he was a communist and would thus subvert Israel. This apparently convinced London of Philby's duplicity and the government decided to bring him to account, with the least embarrassment, and pin him down in Beirut.[30] Philby faced his interrogator as if he knew what was coming but admitted nothing. He was given twenty-four hours to reflect on whether to confess and not be prosecuted or face penury and shame. The next day Philby gave a partial account of his work for the KGB, but asserted that he had broken contact with Moscow after the war.[31] He was not believed and interrogations were set to continue relentlessly until the British authorities had got more out of him. But a change of interrogators had been envisioned, and in the time one interrogator left Beirut and another flew in from London Philby was left to his own devices. On the evening of 23 January 1963, after telephoning his wife, Philby vanished from Beirut aboard a Russian freighter. It has been suggested that leaving him unmonitored in Beirut at this crucial time may have been deliberate in order to facilitate his escape, allowing him to 'fade away'. It may also have been an extraordinary blunder.[32]

The area around Mexico Street, which, as mentioned above, is still rich in traditional and restored houses, becomes chaotic architecturally when reaching Clemenceau.

1   Named after General Edward Spears, Churchill's representative for the Free French based in Beirut. See Zokak el Blat, pp. 90-91, for his headquarters.
2   Saliba 2009, 157-159.
3   el Solh 2021, 25-37.

4   Hanssen 2005a, 247-250.
5   Debbas 1986, 141.
6   Hanssen 2005, 259.
7   Debbas 1986, 90,97.
8   ibid, 88; Hanssen 1998, 62.
9   René Moawad had been a minister in several governments and was voted President at the ratification of the Taif Accord of 1989 (negotiated in Saudi Arabia), which provided the basis to put an end to the civil war. Moawad was a moderate, who believed in the peaceful co-existence of Christians and Muslims, but also in co-operation with Syria. This was considered a betrayal by other Christian factions. The perpetrators of this murder have never been discovered, but fingers have pointed at the head of the Lebanese Army at the time and head of the Free Patriotic Movement, General Aoun, who was anti-Syrian and Israel-supported, and who had refused to attend the Taif conference or acknowledge Moawad as President. However, it may equally have been a Phalange group, Hezbollah or the Iraqis, who might have had grievances or points to prove. The most philosophical explanation was given to the journalist Robert Fisk by a general who implied by a gesture that it was 'Lebanon' that had killed him (Fisk 1992, 641).
10  Fisk 1992, 315
11  Aghacy 2015, 192-3, from René al Hayik's, *Bayrūt* 2002, al-Maghrib: al Markaz al-Thaqāfi al'Arabi.
12  Hayek 2015, 195-7, from Lena Merhej's graphic book *Mrabba w Laban*, Beirut: AFAC.
13  Saliba 2009, 260.
14  Volk 2010, 50-52.
15  Bodenstein 2007, 236-240.
16  Hooper 2013, BBC World Service.
17  Papkova 2016, 187-190.
18  ibid, 190.
19  Bodenstein 2007, 225-227.
20  Baath Party or Arab Socialist Party founded in 1947 by Michel Aflaq. The Military Committee of the organization, led by Salah Jadid and Hafez el Assad, took power in Syria in 1968.
21  Kassir 2011, 484-486.
22  The great-grandfather of the niece of Bechara al Khoury.
23  Chazen, *Daily Star* 2/8/2008.
24  Bodenstein 2012, 209-211.
25  Saliba 2009, fig.32.
26  MacIntyre 2014, 186-203.
27  Philby 1967, reprint 2002, 201.
28  MacIntyre 2014, 218.
29  ibid, 218, 226.
30  ibid, 239-246.
31  ibid, 255.
32  ibid, 261.

# 6. PALACES AND PLACES OF LEARNING ZOKAK EL BLAT, BACHOURA

IT IS HARD TO IMAGINE, walking the narrow lanes and twisting streets of Zokak el Blat, that in the second part of the nineteenth century this quarter of the city was an elite residential and educational centre. Palatial residences (*qasrs*) were built by notable (merchant and political) families, both Christian and Muslim, and schools were established by missionaries as well as literati, many of whom were pioneers of Arab nationalism. A number of Zokak el Blat's street names reflect this history. The district also celebrates the fact that it was the first (under the leadership of the governor Mahmud Nami Bey) to have a paved street (Amine Beyhum); the name Zuqa el Blat translates as 'Paved Street'.[1]

Today Zokak el Blat, like so much of Beirut, is truncated by highways (the Fouad Chebab ring to the north and Selim Salim Avenue to the east). It is thus cut off from what used to be part of its original landscape: the old Ottoman barracks, which became the Serail, and the St Nishan (Armenian Orthodox) church, now considered part of the centre. Permanent residences outside the old city walls appeared as early as the 1820s in Zokak el Blat, but became more common from the mid-nineteenth century onwards with Beirut's economic growth, when the attractions of the space, views, greenery and centrality of the district turned it into one of the most desirable early real-estate spaces of Beirut.[2] Families (and later schools) purchased adjacent plots and formed estates, while other spread out in different areas of the quarter.[3] Monumental mansions surrounded by large gardens, built to suit the topography and sea views where possible, were the initial manifestation of such growth. It is more than likely, seeing the scale of some of these remaining edifices, that competition was a significant factor.

Vestiges of grandeur remain behind high walls or gates and among the apartment blocks, schools, businesses, mosques and religious institutions of this now mixed neighbourhood. Others survive as ghosts of empty plots, but most have given way to modern apartment and office developments.

It is best to discover this neighbourhood as it comes, without fixed walks, savouring its variety and a recent history that is far removed from its origins (see below). Some, however, may at first be drawn to wander in search of ruined *qasrs* or monumental mansions. Three of the most impressive but ruined examples of this early period survive. Qasr Ziade (c. 1870, Hussein Beyhum)[4], now, like Count Dracula's abandoned Beirut residence, towers among cypresses behind a wall. Qasr Heneine stands opposite (late 1870s)[5] and the graceful Qasr Bechara al-Khoury (Patriarcat Street) with a grotto at ground level and a circular staircase leading to the first floor (c. 1890), built by the Greek Catholic merchant, al-Khoury.[6]

Equally imposing were the destroyed Yusuf al Juday (off Patriarcat, captured in a photo of 1864) and the de Freige mansions (pre-1876, also Patriarcat).[7] Less opulent but still grand and surviving are the much-restored Farjallah mansion (c. 1850), now housing the German Orient-Institut on Hussein Beyhum,[8] and Qasr Mukhayyesh (Abdel Kader, 1897/8), built by Amin Pasha Mukhayysh, and still inhabited by the family in 2003.[9] Other mansions include the renovated (Sunni family) plain Beit Mazjoub (Eglise Évangelique, 1850-1860s)[10] and Qasr Kharsa/Batluni (Ahmad Tabbara, 1870s), with circular

Qasr al-Khoury, with the arch of the grotto in the foreground
(Beatrice Teissier)

flights of steps leading up to a tripartite arched lobby. This was the residence of an Ottoman governor and later the Tabbara secondary school.[11]

These residences, made of local sandstone and with partly pitched, red-tiled roofs, were built to accommodate large, extended families and were frequently added to as the family grew, or if the property was sold on (see below for the multiple lives and deaths of some of these mansions). Some floors or rooms were also rented out. The original layout, with rooms fanning out from a majestic central hall, allowed for flexibility. Some rooms were also public spaces used as libraries, meeting places for societies, salons and schools. Stables, shops, storage and servants' entrances were to be found at ground-floor level, with elaborate staircases leading up to the main entrance. While eclectic and of different sizes, mixing classical and Moorish elements in column details, for example, the *qasrs* share certain elements, such as crenellated side towers or high summer chambers (*maysaf*), oculi, central bays with triple arches, arched galleries on one or two sides and fleur de lys decorations on arches.[12] The architects and builders of these mansions are now forgotten, although the Italian known only as Altina is recorded as the master builder of Qasr Ziade.[13]

Whereas the exterior of the mansions looked imposing and elegant, the interiors were more exuberant. Crews of artisans (Italians, Armenians, local) each with their own speciality (tiling, plaster work, coloured glass painting) were employed to decorate elaborate interiors. These mixed 'oriental' elements (e.g. banded stone work, Moorish columns, *muqarnas*, the honeycomb-like decoration used in vaulting as in Qasr Heneine, geometric glass work) were often mixed with western ones (painted stucco work on ceilings such as the floral garlands in Qasr al-Khoury or *trompe l'oeil* paintings in Qasr Mukhayyesh).[14] There was little overall distinction between

Muslim or Christian residences, except for details such as Ottoman symbols (half moon and star) or painted or sculpted Koranic quotes for Muslim homes, or angels for Christian ones. Other details give further clues as to the status of the owner, such as the Freemason symbol entwined with the Ottoman half moon and star of Qasr Mukhayyesh.[15] The prestige of owning such a mansion was acknowledged at the time and sometimes celebrated in odes, such as the one for the merchant Yusuf al Juday's *qasr* (by Nasif al Yaziji), which includes the lines 'a blessed house in which happiness roams ... uniquely built in the regions of the East ... May God protect this house and its builder' etched in a gold ink frieze around his central hall.[16] This part of Beirut, within the orbit of Ottoman institutions,[17] was conscious of its importance.

Schools became landowners in the 1860s and 1870s (as well as functioning in private houses), particularly to the south-west of the quarter. One of the more modest mansions of the period, which was to become one of the most notable, housed Boutros Al-Boustani's National School (al Madrasa al-Wataniyya) established in 1863. This was approximately at the same time that the Syrian Protestant College opened in the neighbourhood and before it brought its sectarianism to Ras Beirut (see AUB). The present-day decay of the National School building (lower end of Boutros Al-Boustani Street) is shaming, for in its heyday it was an avant-garde establishment, headed by one of the leading educational figures of the Nahda or Arabic Renewal.[18]

Boutros Al-Boustani (1819-83) was born a Maronite but converted to Protestantism, as this allowed him greater educational scope and backing at the time, although he distanced himself from this confession and confessionalism in general. He founded his school following the 1860s Druze massacre of Christians in Mount Lebanon. The preparatory school accepted all sects on the principles of tolerance and progress with no proselytization. Languages taught focused more on Arabic and French than English, which led him to clash with the American missionaries.[19] Al-Boustani recruited the best educators he could find, and students came from all over the Middle East, Turkey and Greece, and the school proved inspirational to many later Nahda intellectuals. Al-Boustani was also involved in many literary activities: he was a prolific translator into Arabic, including of the Bible, he was a lexicographer, an editor, an essayist and pamphleteer, a newspaper publisher and the author of a six-volume encyclopaedia.[20] He presents Beirut as a civilized place that loved peace and prosperity and where different races (Eastern and European) shared cultural, commercial and urban values. The advancement of knowledge, ideas of civilization and citizenship were central to his thought.[21] Al-Boustani's son would advance the view that the city of Beirut itself was a civilizing, modernizing entity.[22]

Education together with print culture and the promotion of reading (driven by elites and not the state in Lebanon)[23] were pivotal to the Nahda. Independent presses were set up (the al-Ma'ārif by Al-Boustani and Sarkis), independent newspapers launched (*al Jīnan*, 1870, the *Lisān al Hāl*, 1878) as well as articles and editorials disseminated in official Ottoman papers.[24] The first press associated with Zokak el Blat, however, was the American Mission Press, relocated from Malta in 1833/4, and originally housed on the site of the current National Evangelical Church (1870).[25] The St Joseph Jesuit press was a rival. The American Mission Press predictably concentrated on producing religious works, although it also published linguistic and educational textbooks on astronomy, geography and ancient history and basic educational works by Al-Boustani, Yazijyy and Sarkis (Arabic grammars, dictionaries, vocabularies and poetry).[26] Paradoxically, the missionaries' numerous demands to have the

Bible translated into Arabic was one factor that spurred many intellectual debates on how to best use the Arabic language.[27]

Zokak el Blat became a melting pot of mixed denominational, middle-class intellectuals who knew each other, taught each other and often worked together. Sons often continued what their fathers had started. For example, there were the Greek Catholic al-Yaziyis (father and son, Nasif and Ibrahim). Nasif was a scholar and medical doctor, who taught at the Protestant College. His chief contribution was to Arabic literature and language by freeing the language from its classical constraints, and he opened up the library of his home as a salon for intellectuals. His son created a simplified Arabic printing font and also became a journalist, at odds with those who criticized his father's work, and even Al-Boustani.[28] Another figure was Hussein Beyhum (1833-81), from a powerful Sunni merchant family involved in local politics and state administration. He worked closely with Al-Boustani on a number of cultural projects: he helped found the Literary Support for the Spread of the Arabic Book Society (1868), the Literary Society (1868), the mixed denominational Syrian Scientific Society (1867-8) for the 'spread of knowledge, science and the arts' (presided over by the Druze Emir Muhammad Arslan)[29] and was a founding member of the Islamic Benevolent Society (1878, see Kabbani below). Later in his career he promoted the reform of the Ottoman provincial government in Syria. His son became a Young Turk reformer.[30] Other figures of roughly this generation were the Greek Orthodox Khalil al-Khuri (taught by Nasif Jazijyy, b.1836) and the Maronite Khalil Sarkis (1842-1915). Al-Khuri was an Ottoman functionary but also a poet and literary figure. In the latter role he was involved in the Syrian Scientific Society and was the publisher and editor of the Ottoman-sanctioned newspaper *Hadiqat al-Akhbar*. In his writings he promoted a secular approach, and variously

Arabism, Syrianism, Ottomanism and 'Easternism', but also Syria's historiography, including its pre-Islamic past.[31] Sarkis (whose brothers were all associated either with the missionaries or with Al-Boustani's school) established the al-Mā'ārif printing press with Salim Al-Boustani, then set up his own (Adabiyya), which published Beirut's first independent weekly newspaper (*Lisān al-Hāl*) with widespread correspondents.[32]

Muslim reformers (not secularists) emerged slightly later, partly in the context of general late Ottoman educational reforms.[33] Shaykh Abd el-Kabbani (1847-1935), an Ottoman career functionary, again educated as Al-Boustani's school, founded the Makassed or Islamic Benevolent Society, which ran several schools, including one at his house in Zokak el Blat. This was elementary education, with an agenda to teach girls. Kabbani eventually became Municipal President (1898) and the province's Minister of Education (1906), until he was forced to resign by conservative Muslim clerics. Ahmad Abbas al-Azhari (1852-1926), who taught at Al-Boustani's school, was responsible, with Kabbani, for founding the Ottoman College in 1895, an institution with a more diverse content than traditional Islamic schools (optional English and German), which included an orchestra and a cultural club. It attracted students from Istanbul, wider Syria and the Middle East. Kabbani gained support for the establishment of the Arts and Crafts College (al-Maktab al-Sanai) in Sanayeh. He also taught in a number of other schools and started a book selling business.[34]

As part of a wider circle, the Muslim judge Shaykh Yusuf al-Asir worked with Kabbani on founding the newspaper 'Fruits of the Arts' (*Thamarāt al-Funūn*), aimed at Muslim elites, and revised the Arabic translation of the Protestant Bible.[35] Finally, there was the Egyptian refugee, Shaykh Muhammed Abduh (1849-1905), a jurisprudence expert who formed a salon in Zokak el Blat.[36]

Zokak el Blat was not only a centre of forward-looking educators and there were also plenty of denominational schools which were critical or at least alternative and competitive. The Syrian Protestant College has already been mentioned, and there was the Greek Patriarchal Catholic School (1864-5, Patriarcat Street), Orthodox schools, and the British Syrian Missions School (1860s, off Ecole Évangelique), which became the Lebanese Evangelical School, and now the Hariri High School.[37] There were also schools that were specifically Muslim, such as the Society of Arts, founded by the city's *ulama* (Muslim council) in 1875 which emphasized practical skills and the applied arts, in contrast to Al-Boustani's school. In 1883 an Islamic school, Al Madrasa al-Sultāniyya, was founded with a focus on modern Islamic education and a wide curriculum including French, English, maths, history, geography, Islamic philosophy and painting. The progressive teacher of philosophy, Muhammed Abduh, argued that education needed to be liberal and avoid rote learning, but also that religion should be revived as well as love of the (Ottoman) state.[38]

The district also had its share of religious establishments within it or on its periphery. Many built were built within a few years of each other and no doubt in competition and according to need: the Zokak el Blat mosque (1860, enlarged c. 1900, Amine Beyhum Street), the Moussaitbeh Mosque (1884, south Zokak el Blat), the original chapel of the Greek Patriarchate School (1865), which was within its compound, the American Evangelical Church (1869, Eglise Évangelique), the Greek Catholic Notre Dame de l'Annonciation (1890, Eglise Évangelique), and at the edge of the quarter, the Maronite St Elie (1850s), the Capuchins' Church for Roman Catholics (1870s) the already mentioned Armenian Orthodox Church on Serail hill, and the synagogue at Wadi Abu Jamil, c.1920.[39]

It was perhaps inevitable that this mixture of secularism, religious and educational reform and adherence to Ottomanism while pushing for devolution, and print culture (which reached an ever growing audience),[40] and promoting ideals such as inclusive civilization, local patriotism and homeland, became reactive from the 1870s onwards.[41] The context was one of greater imperialist activity and racial exclusiveness, and it led to the development of Arab nationalism and of the Young Turk movement, as well as to a romantic backlash against modernity.[42]

Mansion building in the immediate area did not stop in the nineteenth century. The Madrasat Fatima az-Zahra (Fatima was the daughter of the prophet Mohammed, and wife of Ali, the first Shia imam) was built in the early twentieth century, after World War I, most probably by a Sunni merchant. It has some of the earlier architectural characteristics: tripartite arches, pitched red-tiled roof, *masyaf* in one corner, a trefoil oculus on the upper floor, but with a new architectural feature of the time such as a triangular gable above the upper floor tripartite arches; it is one block south of Qasr al-Khoury.[43]

## Al-Zaher or Spears House

If curious for history of a different connotation but also of relevance to the Nahda, the visitor might want to seek out the Villa Mezher (off Nakhle Street) also known as the Spears House or Al-Zaher (the red building). This much restored building is a compact two-storey 1920s villa, with a *maysaf*, rectangular verandahs, rounded arches in groups of three on one side and oddly positioned arches on another side, characterized by its red brick colour.[44] One of the villa's claims to history is that it was the headquarters of the Spears Mission to the Levant (1941-2). General Edward Spears was Churchill's liaison officer with the Free French, while pursuing British interests in the midst of the complex rivalry between Vichy France, the Free French and Britain. Spears encouraged local anti-French feeling by colluding with Arab nationalists such as Riad al-Solh and ultimately was instrumental in the departure of the French from Lebanon (officially November 1943, though the last troops left 1945). Spears was made a Lebanese citizen and has the major street named after him in west Beirut.[45] The house became the British Ambassador's residence from the end of World War II to 1980.[46]

It now has a very different role: in 1986 it was sold to an Islamic social welfare institution, the Dar al-Aytam al-Islamiyeh, which is keen to erase its imperialist past. On the occasion of a 2017 art exhibition, the artist Tom Young wanted not only to depict the building itself, but refer to the many people, including General de Gaulle, who had lived, worked and passed through there. This offended the sensitivities of the NGO, who wanted to stick to 'heritage' only images. Spears' face on a painting thus ended up being covered by a primrose.[47]

## Changing cityscape

As anyone walking through this district will discover, it presently offers a jumble of domestic styles: Mandate period apartments, modest high rises from the 1960s and 1970s, indiscriminate concrete blocks, upmarket developments and the occasional shack. The conspicuous development and to some extent the lamentable state of the area's heritage are partly the result of Zokak el Blat's desirably central location. Even in the nineteenth century, it had been home not only to middle-class professionals and scholars, but to working-class and peasant families, including Druze, who cultivated the orchards and plantations that once were a feature of the area.[48] As the district grew (particularly during the Mandate period) with an influx of migrants and the poor (Armenians, Kurds, Shia from south Lebanon) searching for work, affordable middle- and working-class accommodation was needed. Plots were sold on, developed and divided. Gardens disappeared. Zokak el Blat thus became very densely urbanized, particularly to the north-east, while the west and south-west (the more elevated parts) remained more exclusive.[49] Developers joined old families in demolition and development, as well as refurbishment.[50]

The civil war was yet another contributing factor to the district's changing character and face. Before the conflict Zokak el Blat had been a mixed denominational quarter (with a Christian minority), but during the war the area became much more of a contested space.[51] Not only was there war damage

Friendly men sitting by images of President Aoun, the Amal logo and Hassan Nasrallah, the leader of Hezbollah (Beatrice Teissier)

but occupation by various militias (Palestinian, Shia and Kurds, who joined Sunni and Druze groups). Squatters came in with displaced Muslims and militias, and old houses were divided by makeshift walls. Christians were forced to leave. Demolition and construction also continued during this chaos.[52] After the Israeli invasion of 1982 and the formation of Hezbollah, the latter's presence in the district became very visible. The Shia were poorly represented in terms of religious infrastructure, and in 1999 the Husainiyya was built (funded by private donations). This centre hosts official Shia celebrations, distributes alms to the poor and provides medical facilities.[53]

Why was this wonderful heritage so long neglected after the civil war? was a frequently asked question, even before Lebanon's economic crisis. Surveys indicate that multiple factors (already encountered and ongoing) were and are still responsible: joint ownership (where property owners cannot afford to pay each other off), protective rental laws, city expansion plans left in limbo, protective 'heritage' laws with no state support, remaining squatters and, finally and perhaps most significantly, the many permits that need to be obtained from diverse authorities, leading to arbitrariness and illegal payments.[54] In 2013, twenty-six buildings in Zokak el Blat were officially protected and those in a good state were in a small minority.

The decline of some mansions is dismal partly due to their gigantic size, which fated them to multiple lives even when functional. Qasr Heneine, for example, was originally built by a Russian nobleman living in Beirut, sold to the Mezher family, rented out to a Dr Justin Calmette, became the premises of the American and briefly the Dutch consulates (1914-1935), then the residence of Marie Mezher, who ran a restaurant on the first floor while the second floor was rented out. Finally, squatters occupied the *qasr* from 1977-1999. It is now as it stands.[55] Squatters also saw the last of Qasr Ziade,[56] while at Qasr Bechara al-Khoury there was an original connection to the family's antique furniture import business, when the first floor was used as a carpenter's workshop even during the civil war, and a daughter of the family lived there with her servant until the 1990s.[57] In 2019 workmen were clearing parts of it, and in 2021 it was still looking ruinous but with a closed gateway and with motorbikes parked in the driveway suggesting it was partially lived in. Owners can be eager to sell before a building becomes listed, as the pecuniary attraction of real estate development in this desirable area (once permits have been granted and bought) is irresistible. After the civil war the 'gentrification' (a comparatively benign term for money to be made out of demolition) of Zokak el Blat became the norm.[58] From 2000-2013 thirty buildings were destroyed, to be replaced by apartment blocks of twelve storeys or more. These are bought as investments and sold on or used as the permanent homes of the middle class.[59] The process is ongoing and the economic crisis of 2019-21 cannot bode well for this state of affairs.

Others may just want to savour the diverse but rather solemn atmosphere of the district, and observe the symbols of more recent history: political flags and photographs (Shia Amal and Hezbollah), posters, graffiti or the sense of life behind compounds, the life of street corners with small coffee and grocery shops, boys and their motorbikes, the sudden sight of a palace or a well appointed educational establishment, the derelict spaces, the contrast between narrow winding streets and traffic-saturated thoroughfares.

One street that should not be avoided is Boutros Boustani, leading down to Abdel Kader, Kabbani and the Bachoura cemetery. While nearby Basta has the reputation for being a district of upmarket antiques and furniture shops, the wall leading to the cemetery offers its own display of bric-a-brac: musical instruments, ceramics, pots and pans, old utensils, art. This unexpected, modest bohemianism, hints at a change of tone and the vicinity of Basta and Bachoura.

## Bachoura cemetery

The Muslim cemetery of Bachoura is reached by crossing the lung-clogging Ahmad Beyhum freeway, but is well worth a visit. Having negotiated the freeway, a set of steps leads up to the cemetery - possibly the only luminous and peaceful space in this part of Beirut. The hill on which the triangular cemetery stands provides a hint of the expansive views that were once to be had from the hills of Beirut and of the statements made by the monuments of the centre and surrounding *qasrs*. Today the cemetery overlooks areas mostly clogged by residential concrete and modern high rises, but also a minaret, a few period buildings and some of the red roofed municipal buildings of the city centre. But it is the cemetery itself that inspires. White marble graves and tombstones, some tall and majestic, others enclosed, lie in rows interspersed with flowering bushes and small trees. Larger trees are on the periphery. Solitary figures, or couples, sit on the stones or stand reading from the Koran, and the impression is of a place where people come to gather their thoughts as much as to visit a dead relative or forefather. The cemetery most probably has a long history of burials: outside the old city limits it was an obvious location. Its prehistory does not seem to have been investigated, but maps from 1841 and 1857 show pockets of the triangular space already occupied.

A limestone memorial commemorates Ahmed Pasha (1826-85), the Wali of Syria (1875-1876). A map of 1923 refers to it as the 'Turkish' (i.e. Ottoman) cemetery: and Bachoura, because of its topography, has the distinction of having survived Beirut's expansion.[60] Other old Muslim cemeteries, east of the Serail, for example, and the Santiyeh cemetery, close to the harbour, have been swallowed up: the latter by Solidère's 'Waterfront' development.[61] The fate of Bachoura's Roman cemetery has been equally unlucky (see below).

## Bachoura

The walker may now want to retrace his or her steps, continue to Muslim districts southwards (braving more freeways), even attempt to join Damascus Street, or investigate Bachoura. This was once a poor working-class and market district, created from overspill at the interstices of other districts and neglected by the centre. It is now squeezed between main roads and freeways, and parts of it are now being marketed as an upcoming regeneration zone (Beirut Digital District, BDD, Lebanon's 'Silicon Valley'). Much damaged by the civil war, Bachoura was described up to the early 2000s as a 'no-man's land' and in 2010 it became the subject of an experiment by the Department of Architecture and Design of AUB designed to revive one of its *terrains vagues* (seemingly abandoned sites). The Welcoming Design Studio appropriated the derelict Maronite St George's Church (1878) for an installation that was intended to turn the church into a space where locals would interact with each other and the building. Cans were hung over the bell tower, a platform around a giant tree linking garden levels was created as a place to sit quietly, a maze-like room made of bamboos was put at the side entrance of the church to redirect people to the main axis, a panel made of bottles and activated by a pulley was placed at the entrance of the church as a substitute door. Left for ten days, this installation was considered a success by the team in that it attracted visitors and showed that *terrains vagues* can be turned into interesting public spaces[62] but what its lasting effect was does not seem to have been followed up. Art installations set up by artists or academics appear to be a popular means of disguising, drawing attention to and making use of damaged public buildings and the many wastelands of Beirut. Whether these temporary solutions address meaningfully the problem of the latter (suspended in Beirut time) or whether they briefly turn these spaces into mini theme parks is to be debated, but they do show endless creativity and how keen people are to make something of this city. A futuristic vision on BDD's website shows the unfortunate St George's Church (now restored) marooned between what appear to be two supermarket ready synthetic Swiss cheeses (two rectangular eleven-storey office buildings).

The ancient part of Bachoura's heritage, once part of Roman Berytus, is also in the balance. A substantial Roman site consisting of parts of a major cemetery (including sculptures and animal burials), a massive wall, a road, paths, mosaic floors and drains was found in 2016/7 on a plot adjacent to BDD's projected 'masterplan'. The site's future, in the opaque hands of the excavators, the Department of Antiquities, and developers, is presently unknown. Prior to this discovery, parts of the site had already been cleared, while others may or may not be incorporated as a feature of some development (carpark, building).[63] Now (2021) the site stands abandoned and overgrown. This ongoing carving up and demolition of Beirut's Roman remains, now as broken as any ancient mosaic, is par for the course in this city, further obscuring any accurate reconstruction of a plan of Roman Beirut. The extremely thorny question of Beirut's ancient heritage is discussed in the chapter on the Centre (p. 166 ff).

Apart from fashionable looking office buildings, the non-artificial life of Bachoura's poorer streets continues. It is fascinating to wander here: the area is rich in Mandate

Adjoining apartment blocks in different styles, Bachoura (Beatrice Teissier)

period apartment blocks of various styles, some echoing earlier traditional architecture, some with elaborate outside staircases, others with moulded concrete decoration (one of which is both geometric and floral)[64] and a range of cast-iron work. Most are lived in, some restored, some war-damaged. The vast haunting figure of a beautiful young boy lying on his front exploring an Arduino board (by the Cuban-born, now American, artist Jorge Rodriguez Gerada) painted across a row of empty, war-gutted apartment buildings (off Tayane Street) is hugely moving and a poignant reminder of loss as much as of a bright future.

1   Kassir 2011, 114.
2   Hanssen 2005b, 9.
3   Bodenstein 2005, 50-63.
4   Stolleis 2005, 189.
5   ibid, 2005, 193.
6   Bodenstein 2005, 96-97, Mollenhauser 2005, 120-21.
7   Mollenhauser 2005, fig.25, 112.
8   Bodenstein 2005, 56-57.
9   Stolleis 2005, 180; Mollenhauser 2005, 115-118.
10  Bodenstein 2005, 188-190.
11  ibid, 201-203.
12  Mollenhauser 2005, 114-117.
13  Stolleis 2005, 185; see Davie 2003, 64-67 for the names of known masons and builders, both local and from Damascus.
14  Mollenhauser 2005, 117.
15  ibid, 117.
16  Hanssen 2005 a, 167; 2005b 222.
17  Bodenstein 2005, 65.
18  The Nahda was a political and educational reform movement, which although individual to Egypt, Syria and Lebanon, shared certain values such as the promotion of the Arabic language and culture, educational reform, the education of women, sovereignty, the idea of homeland. It led to nationalist awakenings. The movement was pioneered in Egypt by the scholar Rifā'ā al Tahtawi, who spent several years in Paris and returned to Cairo with an appreciation of some of Europe's cultural and social ways. He translated numerous European books and founded a school of languages. (Kassir 2011, 168-169.)

19 Hanssen 2005b, 151-153, 168.
20 ibid, 168-169.
21 Sheehi 2011, 59-60, 63- 74; Hill 2020, 118-119, 124-127.
22 Hanssen 2005a, 227-228.
23 Kassir 2011, 169-170.
24 Hanssen 2005a, 6; Ayalon 2016, 28-29, 82-84.
25 Ayalon 2016, 27.
26 Kassir 2011,183-184; *Illustrated Catalogue…American Mission Press* 1891.
27 Kassir 2011, 170-171.
28 Hanssen 2005b, 165-166; Kassir 2011, 165-167.
29 Hanssen 2005b, 159-160; Hill 2020, 42-47.
30 Hanssen 2005b, 169-171.
31 Zachs 2011, 95-103.
32 Hanssen 2005b, 171-172.
33 Kassir 2011, 176-178.
34 Hanssen 2005b, 171-173.
35 Kassir 2011, 170-173.
36 Hanssen 2005b, 158-160.
37 ibid, 149-151.
38 ibid, 160.
39 Bodenstein 2005, 66-67.
40 Hanssen 2005b, 148.
41 As argued by Hill 2020, 250-255.
42 Hanssen 2005a, 231.
43 Bodenstein 2012, 227-228.
44 ibid, 229-235.
45 Zamir 2005, 811-831; Kassir 2011, 315; Harris 2012, 192, 197-198.
46 Bodenstein 2005, 230.
47 Fisk@indy, 10 May 2011.
48 Bodenstein 2012, 64.
49 ibid, 64, 68-72.
50 ibid, 61-64.
51 Hillenkamp 2005, 214-215.
52 Stolleis 2005, 186-202.
53 Hillenkamp 2005, 224-227.
54 Kögler 2005, 271-277; Krijnen and de Beukelaer 2015.
55 Stolleis 2005, 193-194.
56 ibid, 189-190.
57 Bodenstein 2005, 96-97.
58 Krijnen and de Beukelaer 2015.
59 ibid, 291-293.
60 Stuart and Curvers 2014, 19-23.
61 Hindi 2016, 285.
62 Levesque 2014, 33-47.
63 Battah 2017, 1-37.
64 Illustrated in Saliba 2009, no.3.

# 7. PLEASURE AND PAIN THE CORNICHE AND THE PORT

SENSING THE DENSE, DARK EXPANSE of the sea below the flickering lights of yachts and fishermen's boats is one of the pleasures of flying into Beirut at night. And in daylight few things are more alluring from a plane or a boat than the sight of a glittering sea. Once on land this sight can be indulged in from the luxury of a resort, well placed hotel or high-rise apartment terrace, or from the only accessible seaside promenade in central Beirut: the Corniche.

Having braved the double freeway (with rare traffic lights that barely stop when they change colour or non-existent during power cuts), stepping onto the Corniche, where the sea and rocky shoreline are accessible through railings (from the St George Hotel up to the Manara lighthouse), brings relief, wonder and curiosity. At first, no questions are asked about whose sea this is, who has access to a view that never fails to enliven or bring solace, who in Beirut swims in the sea and who walks the Corniche.

The experience will vary according to the time of day, from the peace and gentle light of the very early morning, when only fishermen or a few joggers are about, to the afternoon and evenings when parts are thronged and the space and mood change almost hourly, and nights when things mutate again and can grow very dark, with only parading shadows and the rotating glow-stick lights of street vendors. Along the way you will encounter landmarks (natural and architectural), receive an introduction to Beirut's culture of display and its undercurrents, and perhaps experience occasional feelings of unease.

## Fame and notoriety

The Corniche was not always the recommended (or possible) promenade that it is today: nineteenth-century guidebooks favoured the walk or ride to the pines (see Horsch, p. 207ff) or an inland trip (via Bliss Street) to the Ras Beirut headland and the Pigeon Rocks. The western seafront began to be developed in the middle of that century with the opening of restaurants around Zaitunay and Minet el Hosn bays and around the port,[1] followed by the first great hotels of the area: the Bellevue, the Hotel de l'Orient (where the early travel agent Thomas Cook & Son's headquarters were), the Hotel des Voyageurs (later l'Univers) and the German Inn (Deutscher Hof). Hotels had private terraces and some access to the sea. Pilots could bring passengers (having cleared customs) to landing stages by the hotels. By the late nineteenth century, sea bathing for the middle classes was becoming more common in outdoor establishments at Minet el Hosn and Medawar (to the east, Mar Mikhael).[2] Postcards showing traditional, four-storey arcaded buildings with red-tiled roofs, remains of old walls, cafés built on stilts overlooking the sea, fishermen and rowing boats suggest a coherence and intimacy to the area.[3]

Development of the promenade started in the early twentieth century and Mandate period of French control. In 1915 broken masonry and landfill from the creation of new roads in the centre were used to widen the seafront. Palm trees were planted, railings installed, and the road became known as the Avenue des Français. By 1922 the coast road south of the old Manara (Bliss Street), an area still comparatively free of habitation, was being built. New hotels opened in the west, such as the Continental (later the Normandy) and the Casino Alphonse. The area became recreational and chic, even somewhat racy, with restaurants, cafés, casinos and a cinema.[4]

A defining moment for St George Bay was the building of the St George Hotel, opened in 1934. Set on the rocky shoreline of the bay, the vast rectangular block of four floors around a courtyard, topped by a water tank, broke with tradition: it was purposefully designed (by Antoine Tabet and French colleagues from the atelier Perret) to reflect new engineering techniques and the Beaux Arts style.[5] The hotel was part of a complex with its own space for yachts, swimming and water sports and became an immediate landmark. It has remained as such for different reasons (see below). The bar, in particular, quickly attracted not only the jet-set, but politicians, journalists, spies and the literati. The famous Lucullus restaurant and the notorious Kit Kat Club were in the vicinity.

Zaitunay Bay was by then a well-known nightlife magnet[6] and beach resorts for an upscale clientele began to define the area.[7] Other types of clubs opened, such as the Bain Militaire (now the Army Beach and Club beyond the Manara), which used to be a popular promenading space, the AUB beach (opposite the lower AUB campus) or the historic Sporting Club (1953), exclusive to the jet-set and politicians. The privatization of the coastline was well under way.

There was a hotel building spree at the height of Beirut's prosperity and cosmopolitanism from the 1960s to the early 1970s: the opulent twelve-floor Phoenicia, with an inner terrace and swimming pool, the Riviera, the Carlton, the Holiday Inn, with a rooftop restaurant and cinema, the New Royal. By this time hotels had started to look alike: rectangular, multi-storeyed, terraced, and with luxurious private facilities. They were places people wanted to stay in.

During the civil war the hotels achieved a different sort of notoriety. As one of the first fronts in the battle for control of Kantari and access to the centre and the port, these hotels and other tower blocks provided perfect vantage points for different militias. The Holiday Inn, in the words of Samir Kassir, was 'not yet open for business but available for war'.[8] The hotels became intensely contested, even with staff and residents inside. The battle for the Phoenicia and the Burj El Murr was particularly ferocious, and fought not only with sniper fire, but with anti-tank rocket launchers.[9] Different militias joined the fray at different times (the PLO with the Lebanese Arab Army, the Lebanese National Movement against the right-wing Phalange and their militias, and eventually the Lebanese Army). Various ceasefires broke down, and in 1977 a truce was declared, with the displacement of Christians from west Beirut and the expulsion of the Lebanese Front from west Beirut, entrenching the division between east and west Beirut.

While many hotels were refurbished and or given new names after the conflict, the cavernous structures of the Holiday Inn (Omar Daouk Street) and the Murr Tower (Fakhreddine/General Fouad Chehab) remain deathly reminders and in post-war limbo. The St George remained.

## West Corniche: from the St George to Dalieh

The St George cannot be missed: it stands partly restored (but empty) in defiance of Solidère's development projects on its property: a sign that used to say STOP SOLIDÈRE has now been reversed and claims that SOLIDÈRE HAS STOPPED. After the fighting its pool, beach and restaurant were at times open. Solidère eventually appropriated St George Bay, and in February 2020 the hotel was apparently given the licence to rebuild, but by July the complex was forced to close due to mounting tax debts.

A close view of the sea when walking along the Corniche is limited and is best achieved going west beyond the St George up to the Manara lighthouse; here railings separate the Corniche from the rocky shoreline. What does this experience entail besides the joy of staring at the sea's colours, hearing waves crash against rocks, seeing a horizon free from concrete and, if lucky, feeling a sea breeze? There will be boys jumping off rocks that are strewn with plastic bottles into a sea where pieces of bread float and more plastic is tossed about. There will be a few fishermen on the rocks, but mostly men sunning themselves with a sound system and possibly a hookah beside them. Some might be brewing tea. The breeze may bring with it a whiff of sewage or of rotting fish. And there are private clubs and resorts: today the coastline of central Beirut is almost completely taken up by these private worlds. The broad rocky promontory of AUB beach and sports area may puzzle the visitor by appearing to be the principal domain of men playing volleyball or other sports, sunning themselves or chatting in groups. Where are the women? There is a small, pebbly public beach just before the Manara, where the poor and migrants seem to congregate. Facilities for ordinary residents or tourists who are not members of clubs are few: there is a café, a family restaurant by the red and white striped Manara and a fava bean seller.

The land side of this part of the Corniche has nothing to offer except traffic fumes, a few cafés, the occasional restaurant, snack shops, high-end hotels and towering apartment blocks. Beyond the Manara the coastline disappears (as does the throng of people) behind the forbidding complex of the Lebanese Army Beach and Club: a vast, protected space with a restaurant, hotel, swimming pool, spa, gym and cabins. This prime, privileged space belies the fact that the Lebanese Armed Forces (LAF) appealed in 2021 for aid for its soldiers (food, fuel, medicine) as well as for equipment. The soldiers' pay (c. US$800 per month) was reduced to virtually nothing by the economic crisis and triggered a fall in personnel. The US government, which is the LAF's prime funder and furnisher of second-hand equipment, duly increased aid.[10] The crisis is ongoing and many continue to leave the military.

Approaching Beirut Luna Park with its Ferris wheel, a few fast food and ice cream outlets and cheap shops bring relief from the barricaded grey stretch of the Army Club. At night this area sparkles in candy-shop coloured neon lights. Beyond Luna Park, the sea seems (and is) further and further away from the pedestrian, as the Rafik Hariri Stadium masks the seaside clubs and restaurants behind it. One of these is the Sporting Club mentioned above, still run by the same family and refreshingly modest (open to families and professionals) in comparison to other clubs. Clubs and restaurants continue to function despite the economic crisis but with a reduced clientele. For the very rich in Beirut the economic crisis is something that is merely talked about.

Savouring the sea from a club, or from the bubble of a hotel or apartment terrace away from the promenade, gives an intense feeling of private enjoyment. This entitlement is very much part of Beirut's brand, but is a privilege of the few (investors, wealthy Beirutis and tourists), and particularly galling to ordinary folk who know that many of the luxurious apartments of the vast sea-front high rises dominating the coastline are investments and empty for most of the year. For most living in the inner city, access to the sea (let alone seeing it) is a remote prospect and requires effort or is even impossible except on holidays.

**To See and Be Seen**

Built for elegant strolling, flanked by crawling traffic, palm trees and colourful benches on one side and sea on the other side, who walks this space?

At first glance it seems refreshingly egalitarian for an Arab country, with a crowd that appears mixed denominational, bourgeois and trendy, with a minority from among the working class and destitute. On an average sunny day, you may see family members wearing the *hijab* or occasionally the *niqab*, families both *hijab-* and non-*hijab* wearing, smartly dressed groups of ladies with surgically enhanced faces, groups of portly men smoking cigarettes, gaggles of girls and the occasional westerner or tourist. Then there are the California-clad female joggers, the bare-chested male power walkers, the headphone freaks, children tearing about on plastic tricycles and actual cyclists. Then there are the show-offs: muscled men in tight Lycra on skateboards, or who jog forwards then backwards for maximum exposure, stunning girls whizzing by on roller blades, carefully dressed younger men strolling with their designer dogs. The poor (migrants or jobless) are there too, but with women and children congregated, as mentioned, on the small pebbly beach by the Manara, with the men, recognizable by their shabby dress and frequently hostile look, strolling aimlessly or leaning on the railings.

Visitors will have to navigate their own space in this crowd, and at busy times like weekends often in zig-zag fashion to avoid adrenaline junkies.

This space is never fully anyone's, except perhaps that of the fishermen who congregate in an area opposite the Ain el Mreissseh mosque and the migrants on the small beach. Yet it seems that everyone wants to own a piece of this space, if only for a short while. The Corniche is turned into a stage by the throng, and its public is not only those who walk there, but the cars that crawl along one side of it. As well as being a zone of diversion, it is thus also one of encounter. All, including those cruising (see Ramlet el Beida below) appears to be tolerated, and identities are exhibited here in a manner that is not accepted elsewhere in a society still regulated by family and sectarian norms. Who therefore is the other in this mêlée?

The most obvious are tourists and migrants, but it could be argued that in this space and in this crowd all who do not belong to an identifiable group are the other to each other. The Corniche is a place of judgement. Amidst the mingling and display there is the sense that much is quietly understood and held in reserve. Much is hidden in plain sight. The gaze, from man to woman, from woman to man, from man to man, from women to women, although not obvious, is complex and ever present. Leaving sectarianism or security aside, who is being looked at (and what for) and judged? The westerner will not be able to interpret this language, which includes 'secret' gestures specific to certain groups (male and female gays, for example), although observation of the body (proper and clothes) is probably ubiquitous.

In terms of male body image, the westerner might observe a bewildering array here: there are the businessmen, *pater familias* types, often revealing a hairy chest and prominent belly; the hip but macho boys and men; the young men in tiny trunks diving off rocks; the soigné men; the fat boys; the severe looking, bearded types; the bandana 'warrior'; the flamboyant gay. Women's agency of expression in this shared public space is more limited, and subject to narrower stereotyping: those who demonstrate their religious affiliation or bourgeois wealth and status (cosmetic surgery, slimness, brand names) modest, 'good family' women and girls, and far less discernible (to the non-LGBT western eye) 'gayness'. These outward parades, male and female, as all over the world often reveal nothing of the real person.

Body image is tyrannical in Lebanon; plastic surgery is almost a rite of passage for those who can afford it, a question of status and of keeping up with one's peers. The ideal is body perfection and desirability, or 'marketability' for women. The evidence of surgical enhancement is everywhere, in the overly bulbous lips and breasts of women, the very straight noses (and bandaged noses claiming the procedure), the fixed, Botox faces, the immaculate pectorals of some men, the unrealistically high and full buttocks of both sexes, and the obviously transplanted hair for the balding. There are also the hidden procedures: the discreetly named 'man surgery', women's 'intimate rejuvenation' processes and the hymen reconstructions.

Women and gay men are probably the most enslaved to this tyranny. Girls are expected to be virgins when they marry, and once they marry to behave with decorum. But it is difficult for many women in Lebanon. The society is undoubtedly patriarchal and laden with Muslim and Christian taboos. For example, stories are rife about the easy-going attitudes of a fiancé, who once married insists on controlling the wife's dress while expecting her to be passively decorative. If working, a woman must be seen to be earning less than her husband. A single mother is severely frowned upon. Violence in the home is rife and child marriages are still acceptable in some religious circles. In theory, women enjoy almost equal civil rights to men, but these are additionally governed by religious affiliation and economic or educational status.

Women are still discriminated against in law. For example, a woman who marries a non-Lebanese cannot pass her citizenship onto her children (or spouse). The girls who run in shorts and tank tops on the Corniche (while enduring lascivious looks and comments) thus exhibit courage, defiance and ideally ownership of their bodies. But there is also a sadness in the ubiquitous plastic surgery which turns some girls into physical clones of each other and in their globalized running gear, making them unwittingly or wittingly 'meat' to men.

There have been successive waves of women's movements in Lebanon since their first mobilization in the 1920s, moving from educational rights and suffrage to welfare and legal rights, to domestic anti-violence and sexual rights. In the context of

Lebanon, these groups can be restricted or at least conditioned by sectarian, political and ideological affiliations. Some groups have been accused of following a western, 'colonial' agenda.[11] This new wave of thinking also includes a call for women to think outside culturally induced arguments of victimhood and to change their own images of themselves and change the world around them.[12] A good introduction to one aspect of Lebanese (and Arab) feminism and sexuality are the works of Joumana Haddad, (published in English 2010, 2012), which are accessible, angry and funny.

Article 534 of the Lebanese penal code outlaws 'sexual activity that is contrary to nature', but this is not regulated unless too blatant.[13] This does not mean that there is no 'street' or societal discrimination, pressure to marry and fear of being harassed or arrested. As a result, LGBT venues and meeting places can be fluid and secret. This can contribute to equally fluid identities, with some of the LGBT groups not identifying with each other ('I am not like them' being a refrain).[14] The effeminate homosexual is part of a group that is particularly discriminated against in Lebanese society (by other males, even gays).[15] Excessively masculine looking women are equally subjected to veiled insults.[16] The politics of style,[17] especially prevalent among the male queer community, is taken to extremes by some who refuse to be boxed in. This may go beyond the muscle shirt, revealing shorts and jewellery into make-up, drag-like accoutrements and outwardly arrogant parading. It can lead to serious homophobic violence.[18] As with some of the jogging girls, there is a sadness and even masochism in the enslavement to type. Yet these groups do not hold back and are extremely vocal about their rights in public demonstrations, as in 2019. The port explosion damaged many of the LGBT safe venues in east Beirut, and this further blow has led to a spike in risky behaviour and drug taking among the community.

## Pigeon Rocks and Dalieh

Walking towards Raouche or the Pigeon Rocks area brings the sea into view again, with the sight up the hill on the land side of the Maison Rose, the old Manara lighthouse and a building that is illustrated in books of architecture: a 1962 Le Corbusier-inspired apartment block with coloured panels and window shades by the modernist Joseph Philippe Karam.[19]

After so much built-up cityscape the sight of the giant stacks of Pigeon Rocks rising from the sea is a wondrous shock and a reminder that this was once a natural, wild coastline with an ancient geological history and a site of human prehistory. It is also a reminder of the beauty of the local sandstone. The rocks were in the past associated with film-set glamour: water skiing, languorous models, boat trips, dare-devil diving competitions and glorious sunsets. But they were the scene of other lives: those of fishermen, of the working class and of weekend crowds. Today the glamour is not evident, but the edge is there despite the hotels, offices and apartment blocks on the land side. The word for visitors is 'don't go there alone at night, 'too many (Syrian) refugees'. It is still a suicide spot. Cafés of various levels of salubriousness line the coast side and are not particularly inviting. Modest families sit on benches, lone men stare out to sea, and a little further on beyond the Pigeon Rocks, besides a fenced off area, visitors may be unaware that they are beside one of the last unspoilt promontories of Beirut, Dalieh. This sandstone headland is now under threat of development. It has traditionally provided a living for fishermen (two fishing ports), and a public recreation and swimming area for working-class families who cannot afford the clubs and resorts that gobble up the coast. The area is geologically and environmentally unique: created by sea and rain erosion, it is the last *karst* (soluble rocks) outcrop of Beirut, with traces of the ancient coastline, terraces, shallow pools, caves and sand dunes. All are important for the preservation of marine fauna and flora, and as a habitat for birds.

The projected development was initiated in 2013-14 by the destruction of ostensibly illegal fishermen's huts and their eviction, with some receiving compensation. Concrete accropodes or breakwater rocks were placed on parts of the site and a tall fence installed from Raouche to the Movenpick resort to the south. A massive campaign, under the auspices of the Civil Campaign to Protect the Dalieh of Raouche, was launched to save the site, with talks, pamphlets, guided tours, banners and boat-rides. Dalieh has been historically owned by Beiruti families, but had been previously exempt from development. With a mysterious change in the law, which also allowed for new rules governing acquisition of land if a hotel is to be built, the exemption no longer holds. In 2015 a second fleet of bulldozers was brought in for another bout of evictions and clearing, although the fishing boats were allowed to remain.[20] The works are now in murky abeyance, and fishermen still fishing, but for how long?

The walker should risk crossing the double line freeway opposite Dalieh to visit the Galerie Janine Rubeiz (1992, off Michelange) on the land side, which displays modern, contemporary Lebanese and Arab art. It has featured artists such as Etel Adnan, Shafic Aboud, Huguette Caland, Lamia Joreige and Dinah Diwan. Some of the latter's work, shown in an exhibition entitled *Wandering City* (2019), evoke remembered neighbourhoods from the artist's teenage years before the civil war (and the family's emigration) in a patchwork of vibrant colours of mostly soft contours, reminiscent of quilts. A visitor might well ask what colours Dinah Diwan would use in her work for the Beirut of today. In October 2021 the gallery was hosting an exhibition by Ghada Zoghbi, entitled, appropriately for 2021, *Pretty Abandoned*. This take on Beirut's *terrains vagues* and derelict projects shows that, by the use of subtle colour and humour, they can be transformed into something mysterious and even appealing.

## Ramlet el Beida

Encroaching privatization again manifests itself further south, at the southern end of the popular working-class beach of Ramlet el Beida, an area that has the dubious distinction of being associated with Israeli bombardment, massacre, terrorism, torture and an escape route for Israelis after their murder of Palestinian activists in 1973. The Chatila refugee camp, where right-wing Phalange militias (enabled by Israel) slaughtered thousands of Palestinians and other migrants in 1982 is in the same municipality. The four-stat Hotel Beau Rivage used to be the headquarters and torture centre of the Syrian intelligence services. In 1983 the nine-storey building housing the French peacekeeping battalion (mostly young volunteers with Lebanese staff) was blasted into oblivion by a suicide bomb that left a vast crater and fifty-eight dead. Another suicide bomber had targeted the US Marine corps a few kilometres away.[21] (This was the year of the bombing of the US Embassy, see Hamra). The war may be over, but the boulevard's reputation as a gay (male) parade ground at night has remained.[22]

The southern end of Ramlet el Beida beach, which has not always enjoyed a salubrious reputation, was chosen as the site for the euphemistically named Eden Bay hotel (opened 2017). It seemed somehow predictable that this Elysian project would be quickly associated with sewage problems. Two engineers from the project were arrested and accused of blocking a sewage pipe after heavy rainwater had caused it to overflow close to the beach. The engineers were later released, with the

Ghobeiry Municipality and the developers blaming each other for the problem.[23] People fear more development. In 2019 'illegal' structures such as shacks, cafés, lavatories, a restaurant and chicken coops - essential outlets for people living in the highly crowded area, were removed on the grounds of hygiene, according to the Mayor of Beirut and the Municipality. A heavy police presence was in evidence.

### East Corniche: Zaitunay Bay and beyond

To the north of the St George Hotel you will pass what was the old Maison de l'Artisan (a landmark modernist rectangular building from the 1960s, defined by a gallery of three-pronged pillars forming arcades supporting a flat roof) now a craft shop and part restaurant. Its original simple exterior and interior style are now ruined, according to one of the original architects, Pierre Neema, by 'pastiche-like additions' after renovation.[24]

Soon after, polished black granite paving and a red sculpture of the marathon symbol announce the modern development and supposedly major tourist attraction of Zaitunay Bay. The

Approach to the Maison de l'Artisan (Beatrice Teissier)

acquisition of the reclamation rights to this site (by passing legal regulations) and its development by Solidère and Stow Capital is yet another example of the privatization of Beirut's shoreline: 95 per cent has already been privately appropriated and is owned by corporate interests, with the remaining 5 per cent under threat. According to Andrew Arsan, this is the product of blatant neo-liberalism.[25]

The Zaitunay Bay complex (by Stephen Hall architects and Nabil Sholam Ltd) is a very far cry from the original bay in its heyday: overlapping terraces encompass apartments, a marina, high-end restaurants and cafés, boutiques, a sea promenade, and at the northern end, a sombre-looking yacht club (with a façade that was intended to be projected, prow-like, but which has been left truncated). On part of a terrace overlooking the bay is a pedestal on which stands a sculpture of a Colt Python 357 Magnum revolver with its end twisted. This is a copy of the famous sculpture by Carl Frederik Reuterswärd made after John Lennon's assassination (now outside the UN in New York) symbolizing non-violence.[26]

In normal times Zaitunay Bay was very much the domain of the rich: security guards, the marina crammed with colossal yachts looking like battle ships rather than pleasure crafts, Sri Lankan or other migrant workers in pink uniforms pushing prams or tending children while the adults enjoy the facilities. The migrant workers are another group (with the refugees) to have been very badly affected by the economic crisis: often dismissed without warning and without pay, or having to work with much reduced wages, their status is more precarious than ever. The economic crisis of 2019-2021 has left this place somewhat, but far from fully, depleted, although by 2021 there were significantly fewer yachts in the bay, and while in the past some locals spent a fortune here just to be seen or to partake in the moneyed atmosphere, ordinary people now just stroll around.

ZAITUNAY BAY

KEUNE
HAIRCOSMETICS

Live your Divinity

Show the world your divine colors.
Discover the four new shades.

Modern synthetic belles of Zaitunay
Bay (Beatrice Teissier)

While now the area is flagged up by advertisements proclaiming 'Zaitunay Bay: Live your Divinity', as the civil war raged the inland part of Zaitunay was, of course, far from paradise. It was a no-go zone except for snipers, but immortalized in the war film *West Beirut*[27] as the location of a brothel run by a legendary madam, Oum Walid. Both sides come to let their hair down and forget their troubles until even the brothel begins to lose its clientele (a mural of a scene from this film is to be found on Damascus Street).

It seems apt that the yacht club should be built on a sea dump from a long-standing accumulation of rubbish (from plastic bottles and nappies to concrete and iron debris) which created an artificial promontory stretching into the sea in front of the old Normandy Hotel. Part of the dump was dredged, reinforced in concrete and reshaped to provide a base for the yacht club (and see below).[28]

## Waterside

Beyond Zaitunay Bay is a large area, part empty, part construction site (over a kilometre long and 550 metres wide at the narrowest point), projecting like a blunted wave over the naval base of Beirut and some of the port. This is the so-called new waterfront project, built again on part of the Normandy landfill and debris from the civil war. It is worth a detour for those interested in barren spaces and brutalist photography. Giant white accropodes flanking the sea on the west side (by a narrow hippodrome-shaped pedestrian and cycle space) gave the place a surreal, intergalactic parking lot feel in 2019. By 2021 the waterside walkway, with a series of scallop-shaped bays projecting into the sea, was open (but not accessible from the yacht club), and equally surreal: a vast, frequently empty, grey lifeless concrete space despite the few discreet couples and fishermen occupying the bays. At the end of the walkway is a large neo-classical entertainment venue (in the process of being renovated) and a bar and evening restaurant (not yet open). The upmarket cocktail bar had been designed as a sunset location, but part of it 'faces east', stated a visitor. The port is to the south-east.

There are a few shacks and indistinct structures in the centre of this complex, including Beirut by Bike, and the whole is crisscrossed by empty roads. It is surely the only place in Beirut that is generally car-free but ironically has pedestrian crossings and traffic lights. Destined for development as a 'Waterfront Park' and business, exhibition and residential area, placards illustrate what is to come: luxury, exclusivity and sea views. 'Be the first,' Be privileged' (to buy) announces a projected Solidère residential development. A welcome spot of green is a small tree nursery near the waterside walk. In 2019 and 2021 the space was still relatively empty (in daylight) save for a few joggers, families on bikes, workers and single men sitting on concrete staring out to sea. The visitor can return to the Corniche via the same walk, or cut inland and join the centre by an avenue leading south and crossing Mir Majid Arsalan into Omar Daouk.

## The port

Approaching Beirut by sea was one of the great pleasures of nineteenth-and early twentieth-century travellers. The sight of the 'white and golden' peak of Mount Sannine when arriving in the morning was one of the 'most magnificent and moving' impressions of all his travels, wrote Lamartine in 1832.[29] When the mist lifted, the city's superb setting amongst pine covered slopes and terraced gardens would be revealed. The old town itself, to the south of St George's Bay, with its crenellated walls, ruined castles and minarets, was deemed 'picturesque'.[30] The northern coastline was then seen as forbidding, with irregular, deeply indented rocks and gloomy caverns.[31] Arriving in the evening, with the rosy tint of the mountains contrasting with the deep blue of the sea, was also a sight not to be missed. Pilots would come to take passengers on shore and bring agents to guide people through customs (a small fee avoided the opening of luggage).[32] Cargoes and crews coming from any epidemic-affected areas would be sent to the 'lazaret' or quarantine station.

The natural harbour of Beirut has, of course, been worked on since the establishment of the Bronze Age settlement (if not before) and work has never stopped since. In the early nineteenth century the quay was decrepit but 'entirely full of people', including those waiting for the monthly packet boat with despatches. In 1860 a wharf was built as the old port was becoming inadequate. With echoes of many subsequent Beiruti planning schemes, a plan to enlarge the port, conceived by a French engineer in 1863 so as to link it to the Damascus road project, had been shelved.[33] After a number of stop and start initiatives, including lobbying for funds locally and abroad, the Beirut-Damascus Railway Company and the local branch of Messageries Maritimes were founded in the 1880s and 1890s. The port concession was given to the Lebanese Joseph

Efendi Mutran (with local families such as the Sursocks and Ayas, buying shares), who then sold it on to the Frenchman Edmond de Perthuis.[34] In 1888 it was reborn as the Compagnie Impériale Ottomane du Port, des Quais et des Entrepôts de Beyrouth (only coming under Lebanese control in 1960).[35]

Work on the port basin started in 1890, with what remained of the Crusader castle, the twin island towers, the old lighthouse and any antiquities razed to create landfill for the quays, with one engineer commenting: 'Beirutis ... consider them ugly, without character.'[36]

A mosque, perhaps once part of the old ramparts on the shoreline, had been renamed after Sultan Abdul Majid in 1840s and left. It has endured many renovations since. Now just north of the souks, it shows where the shoreline once was.

The port was now effectively a private company and in order to capture the hinterland trade, the Beirut-Damascus Railway Company (1897, with a port terminus) and the Damascus Road Company were merged.[37] The Karantina-Damascus line opened with the line eventually going up to Maameltein. Early twentieth-century photographs show the port filled with two and three beamers, fishing boats, barges, steamers and the occasional warship. Huge warehouses lined the docks with stacks of goods ready to be boarded onto trains.[38] Passengers now disembarked onto covered barges from the pier.[39]

The de Perthuis regime, which included new customs regulations and tariffs and a new labour force, was felt as a threat to and a 'yoke' on the guilds and local fishermen. In a flavour of things to come, this conflict led to strikes against foreign and local capitalist development.[40] Nevertheless, by 1905 the harbour was 'good and commodious' and had the reputation of having the only really safe anchorage for vessels of all sizes on the Syrian coast.[41] Steamers operated by various companies, including Russian ones, sailed to and from Egypt and Palestine on a weekly or fortnightly basis. Beirut became the leading port of the Levant and the terminus for lines to the interior. In the Mandate period, however, there were challenges from other ports, notably Haifa (also Mersin) and in an atmosphere of competition with the British, it was suggested that Beirut's port be modernized and that a free zone should be established (where goods would be unloaded without customs duties) and the railway extended from Tripoli to Palestine.[42]

In 1933 the construction of a second docking basin began and the free regime came into effect. By 1938 it was open for business, and with a total of 800 metres of docks, ships of all sizes could be accommodated. With the opening of the airfield at Bir Hassan in 1939 the growth of Beirut was assured.[43]

The massive, forbidding port site, once dominated by cranes, which was a hub for container shipping with a free zone and a commercial duty-free zone handling freight from all over the Middle East and the Gulf, is now partly destroyed. Where incoming container ships and some passengers (nowadays greeted by smog rather than morning mist) arrived until recently is a scene of desolation. This Leviathan was in a constant state of expansion, gobbling up land and sea for new storage facilities, quays, terminals and offices. Then disaster struck. First the port suffered badly from the economic crisis of 2019-2020, when its revenues fell by 30 per cent, with handling down by 40 per cent. A tender was issued for the concession to operate the container terminal, but this was suspended.

On 4 August 2020, a date that will not soon be forgotten by Beirutis, a colossal explosion, felt as far away as Cyprus, tore through the port, devastating it and much of east Beirut. Leaving a massive crater and smashing a major grain silo, it shattered houses, windows and roofs within a radius of eight kilometres. Over two hundred people died, thousands were injured and displaced. This was not (as far as has been ascertained) terrorism, but something equally nefarious: negligence, mismanagement and laissez-faire regulations regarding the unsecured storage of over two tons of highly inflammable ammonium nitrate at the port, thus leaving it open to detonation by fire. The port authorities and others knew of this potential danger, yet nothing was done, virtually giving a green light to the explosion.

Conspiracy theories abound about how and why this material came to be stored at the Hezbollah-controlled port for several years. What has been pieced together by local and other investigations and succinctly gathered together by Charif Majdalani is that a ship with a Moldovan flag carrying ammonium nitrate (a commercial fertilizer), coming from Batumi in Georgia and bound for Mozambique, was diverted for reasons unknown to the port of Beirut. Here the ship was deemed unseaworthy, the Russian owner of the ship refused to pay port fees, the cargo was unloaded (2014), disowned by the owners (Moldova's Rustavi Azot company) and stored in Hangar no. 12. The ship was then abandoned and sunk. Was the real destination Beirut after all? One theory is that some of the people who knew about this chemical filched some of it from the beginning and left the rest. What gives ground to this theory is that if the full amount of ammonium nitrate declared (2,750 tons) had exploded, all of Beirut would have been blasted away.[44] To what extent was this linked to events in Syria?

The actual cause of the fire that detonated the explosion in 2020 is equally murky. The government resigned, but by late 2021 none of the top officials and politicians who knew of the problem have been indicted. Only minor officials have been detained. The government procrastinates and washes its hands of the affair, and even the UN, which has been approached by the judiciary for satellite images of the incident, has stonewalled. What is very clear is the hard push-back against the judiciary.

In October 2021 demonstrations against Tarek Bitar, the judge who summoned the two principal officials in charge of the port (Ghazi Zeiater and Ali Hassan Khalil), turned violent and seven people were killed. Earlier in 2021, the offices of the lawyer defending the port blast suspects (the head of Beirut port, its head of security and the maritime agent of the ship that brought the material to Beirut) was bombed, damaging the building but not the lawyer nor his family.

The port and the area around the silos are out of bounds, but an area to the north-west under Charles Helou Avenue (west of the Charles Helou bus station) remains home to the small Marfa Gallery of contemporary art, surviving and restored among demolished apartment blocks. A local artist, Ahmed, working in wood from his nearby studio (and who miraculously survived the explosion) makes his feelings very clear: 'Tfeh, tfeh!' he says (or I spit on them, those responsible).[45] The scale of devastation is best seen from higher up (for example by asking to climb to the top of a building, if secure): and the scene, although already greatly cleaned up, is still apocalyptic: the shattered silos, drenched in scattered wheat and besieged by pigeons, stand like an abandoned temple among crushed cars, rubble, mountains of metal fragments, window frames, shattered glass, iron railings and rags. In the midst of this flies a Lebanese flag. The site can be seen from the side of Charles Helou Avenue, parts of which are lined with the portraits and names of the dead, including a little girl, Lexou, also illustrated in a commemorative book, *Beyrouth Mon Amour*.[46] Graffito stating that 'our government did this to us' was removed, but keeps resurfacing. A memorial sculpture by Nadim Karam showing a giant angular, lacerated figure holding a dove made from the wreckage of the blast can also been seen. It was unveiled by the port in late July 2021 and while graphic, such a memorial is premature, some people say. The place is still a crime scene.

Beirut port with shattered silos and the memorial by Nadim Karam
(Beatrice Teissier)

On the eve of the first anniversary of the explosion there was
an enormous march through Beirut: 'people want justice' was
the message, which demonstrators sensed would fall on deaf ears.
'There is no justice in Lebanon,' stated a man living through the
aftermath of the explosion, confirming what all thought. On the
anniversary itself there was a memorial ceremony held by the
port, with the names of the identified dead read out (there has
still not been an official tally): it is doubtful that the mellifluous
tone of the actor reading out the names did much to assuage the
anger and hurt of the families. Later that day, the state responded
in the way it knows best: tear gas and water cannons aimed at
a crowd of protesters near the parliament building in central
Beirut. Sixty-six people were injured.

The flattening of much of the area makes the modern
cityscape of Beirut stand out even more from here, notably
Bernard Khoury's towering, black Skyline building, which does

nothing to lighten the mood. The outer panels of the building were badly damaged by the explosion and rather renewing the old, Khoury, ever inventive, devised a way of 'stitching' the skin of the building with simple geometric forms.[47]

Given the strategic importance of the port of Beirut, proposals for the reconstruction of the port have been put forward by many parties: Germany, France, China, the Gulf States and Turkey. So far no deal has been made. 'Beirut will rise', stamped in large black letters on a block of concrete in front of the ravaged scene, is an everlasting message of Beirut's hope, if not faith.

Meanwhile much ambition is invested in offshore oil and gas exploration (one block to the north of Beirut, and one to the south, partly claimed by Israel). Regrettably the first exploration to the north in February 2020 failed to find the reservoir targeted. Unsurprisingly, in 2021 the two parties were still wrangling, with Israel more than ready to take advantage of Lebanon's weakened state.

1   Debbas 1986, 105.
2   Kassir 2011, 219.
3   Debbas 1986, 104-107.
4   ibid, 109.
5   Tabet 1998, 85-86.
6   Kassir 2011, 307.
7   ibid, 307.
8   ibid, fig.100.
9   Jureidini, McLaurin and Price 1979, 5-8.

10 The Lebanese Army's origins go back to troops organized by the French in the early twentieth century and the formation of the Armée du Levant in 1920. The army became autonomous in 1945 (1 August, Lebanese Army Day). The army is multi-confessional and based on denominational ratios. Its commander is presently the Maronite Joseph Aoun. Numbers and resources have historically been kept tight for fear of coups or desertion. During the civil war the army virtually disintegrated as militias took over. Today the army consists of c. 60.000-85.000 troops and is more or less trusted. www.cia.gov; www.lebarmy.gov.leb; Knusden and Gade 2017, 1-22.

11 Kassir 2011, 315-317; civilsociety-centre.org, Lebanon Support 2019.
12 Bayoumi 2014.
13 Merabet 2014, 133-135.
14 Baghdadi 2013; Merabet 2014 *passim*.
15 Merabet 2014, 91ff.
16 Baghdadi 2013, e.g.5.
17 Merabet 2014, 140.
18 ibid, 150.
19 Tabet 1998, fig.19.
20 https://dalieh.org
21 Hammel 1985.
22 Merabet 2014, 166.
23 *Daily Star*, 7 December 2018.
24 *L'Orient le Jour*, 28 November 2014.
25 Arsan 2018, 233-235.
26 Stoughton, 3 October 2018.
27 1998, Director Ziad Doueri.
28 Arsan 2018, 229-230.
29 ed. Berchet 1985, 710.
30 Blondel 1938; Gorton 2015, 35.
31 Murray's Handbook 1858, ed. Gorton 2015, 44-45.
32 Baedeker 1876, 437.
33 Hanssen 2005b, 87.
34 ibid, 89-90.
35 Kassir 2011, 119.
36 Hanssen 2005b, 91.
37 ibid, 95.
38 Debbas 1986, 19-29.
39 Kassir 2011, 119.
40 Hanssen 2005b, 109.
41 MacMillan Guides 1905, 117-118.
42 Kassir 2011, 275.
43 ibid, 276-278.
44 Majdalani 2020, 142-143.
45 *Beyrouth Mon Amour*, ed. Ibrahim, 2020, 48.
46 ibid, 55, by the artist Benoit Debbané
47 Sawaya, *designboom.com*, Khoury.

# THE CENTRE

# 8. PLACES OF COMMEMORATION CENTRAL BEIRUT

THE CENTRE OR *BALAD* OF Beirut – known nowadays also as Beirut Central District (CBD) - is where many visitors will head to, whatever their knowledge of its history, its controversial destruction and reconstruction after the civil war, and its recent shocks. The sight of magisterial buildings, broad, clean pavements, orderly traffic, often empty cafés and few people (adjacent to the traffic-glutted Martyrs' Square) is a surprise from whatever angle of approach. Since the port explosion, the security of this area has been greatly heightened and parts are fenced off.

Two of the best approaches to the centre are from the west: Hamra, as this gives one a feel of Beirut's hilly topography, or the descent from Kantari in order to experience the shock of the clean spaces of exclusive Bab Idriss, where defensive razor wire makes an appearance. On the way visitors will have passed the attractive, plain sandstone Maronite Church of St Elie (or Elias, built in 1907) and the beautiful park of the school of Ste Anne des Soeurs de Besançon (established in 1929-30). Some will also be tempted to see the synagogue of Maghen Abraham in the former Jewish quarter of Wadi Abu Jamil, but this is currently forbidden because of its proximity to the Serail, residence of the Prime Minister. Alternatively, an approach from the south will offer relief from traffic fumes; from the east a jolt in encountering Martyrs' Square after the intimacy of Gouraud Street; and from the north, a surreal experience after the flat, white bleakness of the Corniche coastal highways. The area considered here is east from the Grand Serail to Martyrs' Square, north from the souks to the *tell* (ancient city mound) and south to Riad al Solh Square.

The original centre was a small area (under fifty hectares), partly confined by medieval city walls that were demolished by British bombardment in 1840,[1] general neglect and Ottoman development. The walls, of roughly rectangular shape, had seven gates[2] and enclosed the city on three sides towards the harbour. There was a Crusader and later castle to the north-east to the west of the ancient *tell*, a fortress where the Grand Serail stood, the remains of an old serail to the south-east and Burj (tower) al-Kashef further to the south-east. It is virtually impossible to imagine what parts of the old city centre were like until the early twentieth century: a warren of narrow, unpaved lanes which led organically into one another, small sandstone houses with outside staircases, buttresses, corbelled vaults, and busy street life with livestock herded through to the port.[3] The present layout and architecture is the result of Ottoman and Mandate-period restructuring, religious buildings of multiple lives on top of great antiquity and post-civil war development. Now, yet another layer is being added by post-explosion reconstruction in the CBD.

The city centre was devastated during the civil war. Images of the destruction of central Beirut are not easy viewing: skeletons of shelled buildings, balconies hanging by a thread, collapsed roofs, gaping windows, ransacked shops, empty streets filled with rubble and debris as nature took hold, bodies on the ground, strays and the odd person or child braving the day. Lebanese civil war writing captures the psychological horror of it: the space of central Beirut, itself very small, and once a place of connection, became a vast no-man's land dividing, possibly for ever, the Christian east from the Muslim west. Crossing from one side to another (risking stray or targeted bullets) and staying there. even for humanitarian purposes, could be considered treachery and result in kidnapping and murder.[4] The places people knew become unrecognizable and having lost their previous identity, were given new names such as 'Square of the Dogs', reflecting the feral present. People lost their bearings while surrounded by the sounds of artillery, howling dogs and the occasional scream.[5] But the centre also had a strong hold as a *lieu de mémoire*. In Barakat's *Harith a-miyah*, the protagonist takes refuge (because his old home has been taken over by refugees) in his father's old shop, where he retreats into his own imagination, feeling all powerful and roaming the streets in search of old haunts that gave life to the area but are now empty and desolate. He becomes an explorer and descends into a vault under St George's Cathedral, decides to dig and finds a dead woman leaning against an amphora. He sees her as an object waiting for him and is excited by the macabre discovery[6] but dies reflecting whether he was hit by a stray bullet or an Israeli landmine.[7] Post-explosion writing will no doubt delve into the partly gutted centre.

The old centre of Beirut, however great the damage, was not considered irredeemable. Plans to reconstruct, with different visions of the city's future, were afoot from the end if not before the end of the civil war. One plan of 1991 opted for the total demolition of the historic centre. This was rejected and in 1994 a new plan was instigated after the formation of a joint stock company, Solidère, owned by mostly Lebanese but also foreign Arab shareholders, and in which Rafik Hariri was heavily invested. The company was exempted from taxes for ten years and gained exclusive development rights. It proceeded to expropriate, at unnaturally low prices, all the property of the central district.[8] Opposition was widespread, but Solidère launched publicity campaigns and promoted its vision of 'Beirut, ancient city of the future'. Lavish publications spoke grandiosely of 'strategies of integration', 'extending visual corridors', of turning Foch and Allenby into a 'cultural interface' between port and city; together with the Étoile/Nejmeh Square, these would be the 'catalyst of the city's development' and a 'symbol of historic identity' - as opposed to its pre-war port-related business district (and heart of the city, the author failed to add). Archaeology was to be considered but only to become a theme within the whole.[9] In consequence, vast areas of the centre were razed, while others were reconstructed with modifications, and archaeology eventually ignored or dismissed.

Visitors are encouraged to follow the tourist heritage trail instigated by Solidère, which consists of bronze medallions embedded in the ground with the aim of linking the main public and religious buildings, public spaces, squares and archaeology of the centre in a walking circuit. The approach below is different, with chronological and thematic overviews and the question of Solidère's parcelling out of heritage discussed in the section on Antiquity below.

**Ottoman traces**

Municipal Beirut began to take its present shape from the mid-nineteenth century onwards, when the creation of major landmarks occurred: the Grand Serail (1853), the Petit Serail (1884), the Ottoman clocktower (1897), the Hamidiye fountain (1900), together with the formation and development of squares beyond the city walls (Sahat al/s Sur or Riad al Solh, and the Burj or Martyrs') and the gradual enlargement of east-west and north-south axes. The wharves and souks (both to the north-east and intra-muros) were also being developed at this time, as were other parts of Beirut (such as the Sanayeh and Gouraud area).

The Grand Serail (seraglio, or Ottoman palace) stands on a hill that had long been a strategic defensive position, and in its first incarnation as a military barracks (1853) replaced an earlier fortress demolished in 1840 by the British fleet.[10] From barracks it became the official residence of Fuad Pasha (Special Envoy to Mount Lebanon from 1860), then a prison and medical facility, a ceremonial centre and the present-day headquarters of the Prime Minister. At the time, the Grand Serail (known as such from 1880)[11] was the largest building in Ottoman Beirut: with two storeys and flanked by symmetrical wings, identical windows and oculi.[12] It became a statement of civic architecture and of Ottoman state power.

The Grand Serail has retained its sober façade and looming presence, while also having undergone a number of facelifts. The entrance changed from its original double staircase leading to an arched neo-Islamic style portico with the Sultan's *tughra* (calligraphic monogram) above to a projecting double balcony with arcades during the Mandate period. A third level was added in the post-civil war reconstruction.

In 1897 the prestige of the space was further enhanced by the addition of the clocktower. The Governor of Beirut had written to Sultan Abdul Hamid II's Court Chamberlain stating that, given the number of foreign institutions that had clocktowers with bells, Beirut was in 'urgent need for a general clock which determines the religious time of the Muslims'.[13] Yussuf Aftimus was chosen as the architect and deployed his trademark eclecticism: the twenty-five-metre campanile-style tower is made from a variety of stones - local sandstone and limestone, basalt from Damascus and red stone from Deir el Kemar, with different window types, *muqarnas* (honeycombing) detailing above the entrance, *mashrabiya* (latticed windows), variegated stone work and crenellations at the top.[14] The tower was inaugurated to commemorate the anniversary of

Sultan Abdul Hamid's coronation with all the ritual pomp of Ottoman public state openings.[15] It immediately became part of the skyline of Beirut and is now dwarfed but intact

Despite landscaped gardens, the Serail area, even in 2019, was not a place of public relaxation. In 2021 the whole area around the Serail and south of Weygand was off limits to anyone except employees, who had to show their papers. An intrusion into this ex-Ottoman space is the Mandate-period St Nishan Armenian Orthodox Church, built in 1934, almost as a gesture of defiance to the old Turkish state and its genocide. The church has white limestone facing with some Art Deco features and mosaics in the apse, squinches and above the door.

## Martyrs' Square

Nejmeh or Étoile Square (may be) where visitors head to for the experience of a shared public space in central Beirut, but the alien atmosphere disappoints. The real heart of central Beirut used to be the Burj or 'tower' (present-day Martyrs' Square), its name derived from the remaining Crusader watchtower and later fortress, demolished in 1874. Once an area just outside the city walls, it was filled by gardens on the site of the palace of the Druze Emir Fakhr al-Din II (see below). The area then became the dumping ground for Russian, English and French artillery (hence its later French name Place des Canons).[16] Turning the area into a formal square dedicated to Sultan Abdul Hamid was first envisaged by Ahmed Pasha (Governor of Syria) and Fakhry Bey (head of the municipality) in 1884.

A municipal government building, the Petit Serail, had also been commissioned to the north of the square, to replace a former, damaged palace, named after Emir Assaf. This building, inaugurated in 1881, differed greatly both in scale and tone from the Grand Serail; it was more graceful, with much shorter wings, a neo-Baroque pediment and a marble arched gateway leading to an inner courtyard. Despite the architectural eclecticism of these municipal monuments, they blended in with their surroundings. After Beirut became a provincial capital the Petit Serail became the seat of the Governor General.[17] It was destroyed in 1950.

A postcard of 1900 shows the square with the Petit Serail and an attractive *fin-de-siècle* formal circular garden with a fountain and kiosk encircled by iron railings[18] and horse drawn carriages waiting for custom. Unfortunately the original garden of the square was razed in 1921 to make place for the Beirut Fair and in 1925 was planned as a rectangular French-style garden and terminus for carriages, trams and eventually taxis and buses.[19] The area later became associated with entertainment: street cafés, restaurants, cinemas, hotels from chic to seedy, and in parts prostitution.[20] Filled with hawkers, shopkeepers, people going about their business or looking for diversion, all life was there.

Initially called Hamidiyeh, the square was renamed Liberty or Union Square after the Young Turk revolution of 1908[21] but became notorious as the site of the execution in May 1916, for treason, of a cross-confessional group of Lebanese nationalists (poets, journalists, activists) not all necessarily united in what allegiance Lebanon should have in the future. Turning the martyrs' graves into a site of commemoration would have been too contentious, and as different narratives have it, the martyrs' bodies were either thrown in a ditch and later retrieved to be taken to the Druze cemetery, or immediately taken to the cemetery, which houses them in a separate enclave (see p. 70).[22] A committee was nevertheless formed to create a memorial to this event and *Les Pleureuses*, a sober and dignified monument designed by the Maronite artist Youssef Hoyek was the result. Erected in 1930, the monument showed two statuesque women (one Muslim, one Christian) similarly robed but with different headdresses, cast as mothers joining hands over a cinerary urn. They respectively had a cross and a stylized *shahada* (the Muslim profession of faith) carved on their chest. They stood on a block on which there was the image of a cedar tree and two fasces (a popular symbol of strength and unity for nationalist movements derived from Rome and associated with fascist Italy) supported by a podium.[23] At the time it was the centrepiece of the square (renamed Martyrs' Square in 1931), surrounded by palms and other trees and partially enclosed by an iron fence.[24]

This solemn piece of art proved unpopular: it was associated with the French Mandate and/or considered idolatrous, unmanly and weak,[25] although the Suffragettes were one group who used the memorial as a rallying point for International Women's Day.[26] The monument was vandalized with a hammer by one Selim Sleem in 1948; the act was not condemned by the government at the time and the monument stayed where it was for a while, until its top (head and shoulders of the women) was then mysteriously removed leaving the lower part. But the top part was not destroyed and was found again by accident in a warehouse in 2001, when it was taken to the Sursock Museum, where it now stands in the courtyard.[27]

*Les Pleureuses* by Youssef Hoyek

A new monument was now required but the transition from the 1930 monument to the present day one was not straightforward. The Martyrs themselves became the subject of ideological debates: were they representative of Arab nationalism or of the Mandate-period government they opposed? Meanwhile the date of martyrs' day was changed from 2 September (Mandate period) to 6 May, the date of the executions. An international competition was launched for a new design and opinions varied over scale, positioning and iconography. Personal involvement in this process was displayed in an extravagant architectural and figural design by the engineer and architect Abdel Baki, President of the League for the Commemoration of Martyrs. In 1957 a scaled down version of the original, showing two muscular giants holding up a torch (in Soviet style) was chosen but never made. The present monument by the sculptor Marino Mazzacurati, erected in 1960 (after the 1958 civil war), is a design modified from Abdel Baki's original. It depicts four bronze figures: Liberty holding a torch beside a young man, and two struggling males attempting to rise from the ground.[28] Theoretically representing concepts such as heroism, strength, liberty and victory, it is difficult to see how the utterly western, dated, socio-realistic, quasi-fascist iconography of this monument is a better symbol of the martyrdom and suffering of Lebanon than the original. Its incongruity was pointed out at the time,[29] and it has stronger associations with dubious state power than with human struggle against injustice.

Today Martyrs' Square is a far cry from the busy human meeting place it used to be and is a lamentable space yielded to traffic, yet while approaching the monument is hazardous, it is worthwhile to witness its dramatic, carefully curated, scars of war. Martyrs' Square was very much in the crossfire between the two sides and their militias during the civil war and the memorial was left bullet- and shrapnel-ridden. After the war, President Hariri decreed that the statues should be restored, to honour not only the martyrs of 1916 but the victims of the modern conflict. Damaged as they were, the statues themselves had become martyrs, announced the press.[30] They were painstakingly restored, leaving bullet holes and one arm blown off by shrapnel (while another. arm was reattached), and eventually put back in place.

## Riad al Solh

Another square or rather triangular space that has its antecedents in the Ottoman period is Riad al Solh. Known originally as Sahat al/s-Sur ('high wall'), the area was originally wedged beside the old town wall and developed at the conjunction of two streets leading from Zokak el Blat and Bachoura to the centre. It was also accessed via Bab Yacoub from the south. In the second half of the nineteenth century it developed predominantly as a Muslim working-class space and it was here that the Hamidiye fountain was erected in 1900, in honour of the twenty-fifth anniversary of Sultan Abdul Hamid II (see p. 68). The area developed its own character, becoming the site of ceremonial processions and festivities such as circumcisions,[31] with souks, a hammam, coffee houses, and, due to a telegraph office, a centre of information and gossip.[32] The area's individuality began to be lost when it was redeveloped in 1949. It was renamed Riad al Solh Square in honour of the Lebanese Arab nationalist, architect of the National Pact (with Bishara al-Khoury) and first Prime Minister of Lebanon after independence, Riad al Solh (1894-1951). He was gunned down in Amman in 1951 by the Syrian Social National Party in retaliation for his administration's execution of Antun Saadeh, the intellectual anti-denominational activist and founder of the Syrian

Nationalist Party, who had long been considered a source of dissent in Lebanon.[33] A statue of Riad al Solh (designed by Marino Mazzacurati) was erected in the square in 1957.

## French imprint

The Mandate period layout between these squares is a combination of late Ottoman planning, Haussmann-like development and Solidère's impositions.

Modernizing streets and turning the centre into a showcase for business and administration was a priority for the colonial government. So too was the branding of French names on the urban environment. The area around Foch-Allenby and Weygand continued to be cleared and became a new governmental and office district, with imposing avenues and buildings made of reddish sandstone, such as the Palais Municipal and the Parliament building. A new square, the Étoile, was created. A feeling that wide boulevards do not sit well in Beirut remains; but at the time they allowed for swift military mobility.[34] While the scale of the monuments may have been shocking to the populace, there was a certain harmony, as there had been during the Ottoman period, in the overall use of sandstone[35] and in the eclectic detailing of the architecture of which there were echoes throughout developing Beirut.

The Municipality or City Hall and the Government building are the two dominant civic monuments of the centre. The Municipality building (1924-5) on Weygand Street was designed by one of the most prolific architects of the late Ottoman, Mandate and early Independence periods, Yussuf Aftimus, whose work has already been encountered (Hamidiye fountain, Serail clocktower). The eclecticism and variety of his architecture were deliberate, and partly the result of his widespread travels and studies in America and Belgium.[36]

The palatial yet fortified looking (side towers, crenellations) Municipality building, for example, is characterized by a Venetian-Moorish, or neo-Mamluk style in contrast to the Barakat Building,[37] built at the same time (see p. 199). Another example of the playfulness of Aftimus' style is the Grand Theatre (built 1920s, opened 1929) at the corner of Emir Bashir and Syria Streets. This has a neo-Moorish horseshoe arch entrance and rectangular and pointed arched windows with small balconies, but fantasy is particularly evident in what remains of the interior decoration of this graffiti-laden, derelict building (to be developed by Solidère), with its coloured glass ceiling rotundas with floral and geometric patterns and internal cupolas of geometric design.

The Government building (1934), by Mardiros Altounian, on the other hand, shows the influence of a specific style: that of the École des Beaux Arts, where Altounian had trained. He had been commissioned to create a monument inspired by 'the Lebanese style'.[38] Whether this was achieved is debatable, but the severe building, dominated by the perpendicular, is tempered with neo-oriental detailing (*muqarnas* or honeycombing, arched windows and recessed arched entrances). Altounian was also responsible for the Étoile clock, which is even more rigid, but perhaps this is in part to distinguish it from Aftimus' Serail clock, and for the refashioning (1932) of the old Debbagha Mosque, now known as the Abou Bakr al-Siddiq Mosque. The attractive building shows all the characteristics of Altounian with Ottoman, Mamluk and Art Deco elements.

The incongruous radial plan of the Étoile (Nejmeh Square), designed by Danger Frères, which completely changed the ancient orientation of the centre (see below), was created by the clearing of the warren-like ways of the old town to the east and south. Originally eight branches had been planned, but only six were built, in order to save the Greek Orthodox, Greek

The Étoile clock by Mardiros Altounian (Beatrice Teissier)

Catholic and Maronite cathedrals, the Nuriye chapel and the Mosque of Mansur Assaf.[39] The response to this transformation was mixed: negative from the intelligentsia, but not from the merchant families or the religious establishment.[40] This work resulted in a generally severe space, often empty and lacking life, except when holding certain festivals or at New Year. In 2021 it was not accessible to the ordinary public.

The often funereal atmosphere of sanitized central Beirut has been mentioned. On numerous occasions, however, Martyrs' Square and other parts of the centre have resonated with the sound of political chants and flag-waving crowds, and have provided a sometimes confrontational ground for a series of notable demonstrations. The centre's pristine veneer has been tarnished more than once by graffiti and smashed windows. One of the most memorable demonstrations, dubbed the 'Cedar Revolution', was that of 2005, triggered by Rafik Hariri's assassination. Thousands marched for the withdrawal of Syria from Lebanon (achieved in 2005) and for the resignation of the pro-Syrian President, Emile Lahoud. Martyrs' Square was occupied for two months, with the establishment of a Freedom Camp. Hezbollah countered, but on the whole the protests were non-violent. From 2006 to 2008 there were protests against the US and the Saudi-backed government, and in 2011 rallies against confessionalism and the sectarian political system.

In 2015-16 a major protest was sparked by a long-standing waste disposal crisis. The Naameh waste plant south of Beirut was closed by activist action in 2015 after years of complaints about its toxic effect on the local population. There was no provision for a substitute site. Waste collections were halted and mountains of rubbish accumulated in the streets of the city: the stench and vermin became unbearable. Landfills were created at Burj Hammud and Costa Brava, near the Rafik Hariri airport, and collections started again. Yet the mismanagement of private company waste contracts and the scale of the problem resulted in no-one bidding for new contracts offered by the state, and the problem endured. A contract was finally given, in secretive conditions, to Ramco and Atlas in 2018. Meanwhile the rubbish crisis remains: 75 per cent of Lebanon's refuse goes to landfill and much of it is burnt. Even when it is collected, the streets of Beirut (not the centre) can still be littered with overflowing black rubbish bags, while dumping and burning in the countryside is endemic.

Longstanding issues also came to the fore in 2015-16: electricity blackouts, water shortages, ineffective leadership, corruption, police brutality. These protests became violent, and the Beirut Medinati (Beirut My City) movement, which became a party, emerged in response. Its goals were responsible civic governance, covering waste management, green spaces and affordable housing. Despite having some electoral success, this organization has remained one of many which are not part of the establishment. The protests engendered a huge burst of street creativity.

The most recent, and the most volatile, protests have been those of 2019-20, sparked by the planned taxing of the free WhatsApp service and the economic crisis. Demands quickly escalated to include access to decent jobs, a functioning economy, acceptable salaries and health care provision, as well as the perennial calls against corruption, sectarianism, lack of transparency and the Taif agreement (1989, which enshrined the sect-based political system).[41] Protests ranged from peaceful human chains, street theatre, concerts, street art and graffiti to storming barricades, smashing windows, looting and setting fire to debris and to the Central Bank. Street art has become a potent form of resistance and is now proliferating: visitors cannot avoid noticing wall art (many examples along the concrete entries of underpasses and freeways) or on street walls by professional and non-professionals alike. The police countered with batons, rubber bullets and water cannons.

As the conflict descended into violence, sectarianism came into play. Demonstrations were not confined to Beirut, but took place in Tripoli, the Beqaa, Tyre and elsewhere. Prime Minister Saad Hariri resigned in January 2020 and was replaced by the unpopular engineer Hassan Diab. The latter resigned after the port explosion of August 2020, to be replaced by Hariri as interim PM once more. Since the explosion there has been a flurry of aides, diplomats and envoys from Europe and the US offering aid in return for reforms, but the factions of the President and the Prime Minister, and their proxies, have held their ground in refusing to yield over voting rights in any new parliament. In late June 2021 protests erupted in Tripoli, Beirut and Sidon chiefly against the currency's tumbling value, inflation at 84 per cent (while the black market thrived) and dire living conditions (lack of fuel, electricity, medicines), all compounded by the Covid-19 pandemic. In Tripoli protesters and police were injured. In July power stations were closed, while the EU and others dithered on whether to impose sanctions on the ruling elite. The country remained without a government. 'Beirut is days from a social explosion,' headlines announced in July 2021. On 15 July 2021 Saad Hariri quit once again after failing to reach a deal with the President over forming a government. Finally, on 10 September the Sunni tycoon Najib Mikati, who had previously served in the role, was made Prime Minister. 'Reforms, under him? He's a gangster, like the rest of them … Same old, same old,' people say.

Visitors may be more than bewildered: how could the people in charge let the country disintegrate this far? they might ask. 'It will get much worse before it gets better,' say locals, whose resilience, unknown in most of the West today, has long been tested. Conspiracy theories proliferate: 'This is surely deliberate, they want Lebanon to be taken over, but we don't know by whom'. 'There is an evil will afoot.' 'We are going to be eaten up, they want us to surrender.' 'We have been abandoned, it is going to be a free for all.' The spectre of Israel and the US hangs heavy for some, while for others it is Iran and Russia.

Whatever the year of protest, the demonstrators' slogans reflect Lebanon's enduring problems with its ruling class: 'You have stolen my dream', 'You are the ones who stink', 'Some rubbish should not be recycled', 'Je me révolte donc je suis' (a quotation from Albert Camus). A Lebanese friend visiting London in June 2021 was astonished at the anti-vax demonstrations: 'In Lebanon we demonstrate for food, electricity, clean water, a decent government. Here they demonstrate against something that all the world wants!'

**Back to life?**

Whether the 'lobotomised phoenix' (in the phrase of Naccache)[42] that is the new centre of Beirut will ever sear itself into peoples' memories as a true centre and place of life and connection is still a very open question.

---

1  Sidon and Beirut were shelled in 1840 by the British and Austrians in a war against Muhammed Ali, the powerful Governor of Egypt (1805-48), who sought to take over the Ottoman province of Syria. He invaded Syria in 1831-33 but was defeated at Acre. He agreed to withdraw from Syria in return for hereditary rule over Egypt and the Sudan.

2  West: Santiyeh, Idriss; south: Yaqub, Derkeh, Abu Nasr; east: Seraya, Dabbaga.

3  Debbas 1986: 47-49.

4  Hayek 2015, 75-79 cf. Etel Adnan's Marie Rose, 1978.

5  Aghacy 2015, 182-183, 185.

6  ibid, 180-181.

7  ibid, 187.

8  Shwayri 2008, 89.

9  Saliba 2004, 51-55.

10  Debbas 1986, 95.

11  Hanssen 2005, 242.

12  Debbas 1986, 97.

13  Hanssen 2005, 243.

14  Debbas 1986, 97.

15  Hanssen 2005 238, 245-246.

16 Volk 2010, 53.
17 Hanssen 2005, 243.
18 Debbas 1986, 68-69.
19 ibid, 69-72.
20 Khalaf 2006, 201.
21 This was a rebellion by the Young Turks, a reform movement of the early twentieth century that sought to replace the absolutist Ottoman rule of Abdul Hamid II with a constitutional regime and the reinstatement of the Ottoman Parliament.
22 Volk 2010, 49-50.
23 ibid, 56.
24 Debbas 1986,74-76.
25 Volk 2010, 68, 75.
26 ibid, 68.
27 ibid, 67-69.
28 ibid, 76, 97-98.
29 ibid, 100-103.
30 ibid, 109-111.
31 Debbas 1986, 88-91
32 Hanssen 1998, 61.
33 In the context of the humiliating Arab defeat of 1948 and a coup d'état in Syria, Sadeh, as leader of the SSNP, arranged a revolt against the Lebanese government in 1949, accusing it of having helped precipitate the disaster in Palestine. He was accused of wanting to overthrow the government and collusion with Israel (!) and summarily executed in 1949 (Kassir 2011, 451; Trablousi 2012, 115-116).
34 Khalaf 2006, 78.
35 Kassir 2011, 287.
36 Saliba 2004, 122.
37 ibid, 122.
38 ibid, 123.
39 Kassir 2011, 281-282.
40 Khalaf 2006, 79.
41 The agreement made in Taif (Saudi Arabia) in 1989 formed the basis for ending the civil war. Its general principles were that Lebanon should be a free and sovereign country; that it should be Arab in belonging and identity; that it should be democratic, with freedom of expression and belief, upholding social justice and equality; that its people were sovereign; that it should have a free economic system with development as the mainstay for the nation's unity and stability; that efforts for social justice should be made; that there should be political and fiscal reform; that Lebanon should be united and belong to all Lebanese. Its aims were to abolish sectarianism (with no time frame). Parliamentary seats were to be shared equally between Christians and Muslims, proportionally between each denomination and district. This, according to most people, has led to stalemate, rivalries and corruption. The Maronite President became a figurehead, and the power of the Sunni Prime Minister was enhanced.
42 Nacchache 1998, 141.

# 9. THE RELIGIOUS CITYSCAPE CATHEDRALS AND MOSQUES

THE CLUSTER OF MIXED CHRISTIAN and Muslim religious buildings (with the exception of the vast Muhammad al-Amin or Hariri Mosque) are the monuments in the centre that give a flavour of Beirut's post-antique and in some cases antique history. Many were built on earlier religious foundations, and restoration, reconstruction and even rediscovery after the civil war has allowed insights into Beirut's successive civilizations and townscape.

The Ottoman period St Elias Eastern Greek Catholic Cathedral, to the east of Nejmeh Square (1849, 1863, originally a convent) and the St George Maronite Cathedral (1884-94), south-east of the square, are examples of nineteenth-century Beirut's miscellany of architectural styles. St Elias was built in a neo-Byzantine style, with many subsequent changes to its exterior, whereas the Maronite Cathedral, built on a basilica plan and on the site of an earlier Maronite church, has an incongruous neo-classical façade inspired by the Basilica di Santa Maria Maggiore in Rome. The latter appears dwarfed by the minarets of the al-Amin Mosque, even though the minarets are ostensibly the same height as the Cathedral's campanile. Both cathedrals hint at the past of the area in their re-use of Roman columns; St George sits on part of a Roman street and also incorporates Hellenistic and Ottoman structures within its compound. Its interior is light and airy, with a coffered

The St George Greek Orthodox Cathedral with ruins in the foreground
(Beatrice Teissier)

ceiling, a gallery supported by columns, stained glass windows and mosaics, with an ornate canopy over the main altar. The interior of St Elias is beautifully sober with banded stonework, marble podia and altar and large icons.

The St George Greek Orthodox Cathedral (adjacent to the Garden of Forgiveness, see below) brings visitors deep into Beirut's history and is one of the more rewarding and attractive monuments to visit in the area. The rather garish frescoes of the interior of the present cathedral contrast with its elegant, restrained sandstone exterior, slim columns, pointed and rounded arches and oculi. The cathedral is on the site of one of Beirut's fifth-century Christian churches: the Anastasia and the Cathedral of Eustathius (Bishop of Beirut), which may have been adjacent to the law school of Berytus (see below). Contemporary sources describe the magnificence of this ancient cathedral, with 'gleaming columns' and images 'to seduce the pagans'.[1]

Other early Christian churches of Beirut included the Theotokos, with depictions of Adam and Eve's expulsion from Paradise, the Church of St Jude, and martyria (holy burial sites).[2] Historical sources also suggest that the atmosphere of early Christian Beirut would not have been too alien to the inhabitants of the later city: there was a lack of conformity around religious beliefs (non-Christian, Christian, schisms within Christianity)[3] together with a multiplicity of languages and a range of civic and ethnic identities.[4] The Cathedral of Eustathius was destroyed in the momentous sixth-century earthquake which damaged so much of Beirut. The cathedral subsequently had many reincarnations: rebuilt in the twelfth and the mid-eighteenth century after another earthquake, rebuilt again in 1772, modified in 1783 and in 1910. After civil war vandalism and shelling it was reconstructed from 1998 until 2003 when it reopened.

One of the bonuses of the present St George Cathedral is its crypt museum (inaugurated in 2011) based on *in situ* excavations prior to the reconstruction of the church. The walking circuit is accompanied by explanatory panels and display cases. There was occupation from the Hellenistic period onwards, but the Roman and Late Antique/Byzantine is in evidence through the main artery or *cardo*, various mosaics, column bases and a drain), and the medieval period best represented by painted pillars, an apse and stone paving over a necropolis. There are Mamluk period burial sites around and burial vaults of the Ottoman period.[5] An additional gift of the cathedral area is the small chapel in an adjacent garden on the site of the historic Sayyidat al-Nouriyyeh (Our Lady of Light) shrine. It is home to icons, including a 'miraculous' early seventeenth-century representation of the Mother of God.

## Muslim landmarks

The early Muslim Caliphate[6] from the time of the Arab conquest in 635 AD has regrettably left few traces in Beirut. It appears from contemporary accounts that Beirut was swiftly conquered - apparently having no defensive walls at the time - and it remained vulnerable to Byzantine attacks from the sea. As a frontier outpost, Beirut was turned into a naval base, and by the eighth century it had acquired the status of *ribat*: a fortified station where it was a religious duty to serve against the enemy (the term *ribat* was later used to mean fortifications).[7] It was thus firmly set within the Muslim fold. The population was mixed: Muslim commanders, soldiers and sailors and families once it was secure, Jews, Christians and Copts.[8] In the Abbasid period there was influx of religious scholars and their families, because Beirut had by then acquired a certain cachet not only because of its status as a *ribat*, but because of the presence of the scholar 'Amr al-Awzai (707-74). Awzai had moved from Damascus to Beirut to escape political turmoil.[9] He settled in the city as a teacher but became a mediator between the people and the Caliph, defending the rights of soldiers, of Christian in the mountains (who had been collectively punished after a rebellion) and of people in Mecca. He had the reputation of being a 'man of the people', fair, pious, ascetic and not corrupt.[10] By the ninth century he was seen as a saintly figure, and the remains of his *zawiya* (gathering place for followers or students), marked by an Ottoman inscription (in Souk al-Tawileh, near the Al-Omari Mosque), were visited and candles deposited there until the end of the Ottoman period.[11]

Awzai's reputation and those of his students, who became scholars in their own right, as well as the fact that Beirut had been visited by companions of the Prophet, not only contributed to the economy and status of the city, but also helped fashion it into part of the Muslim sacred landscape.[12] Awzai's tomb and shrine are in the mosque of the poor southern suburb of Ouzai. Visitors who do not know of the importance of this figure can easily pass by the small mosque, while having looked in amazement at spectacular murals by world-class artists, painted on the concrete blocks of Ouzai, where the inhabitants live with no running water, piles of rubbish and unpaved streets. This incongruous, provocative mural project, named 'Ouzville' was the brainchild of a native of Ouzai, Ayyad Nasser, who thought it would boost the local economy. The local economy is still waiting and the locals are either ignored or stared at as curiosities when art and architecture students take note of the colourful murals.

The archaeology of the Caliphate period in central Beirut is limited: there is a possible Ummayad-era mosque in the southern part of the old town, and a bathhouse that had its origins in the Hellenistic period and still used in Mamluk

Restoration of the partially damaged Al-Omari Mosque (Beatrice Teissier)

times.[13] By the tenth century the city had a fortress and well-fortified walls and was subject to Damascus.[14] The late tenth to the late thirteenth centuries were periods of conquest and reconquest of the region by the Abbasids, Byzantines and Fatimids. After the Byzantines were defeated at Manzikert in 1075, the advent of the Crusaders ushered in another period of instability for the Levant. By the early twelfth century they had occupied Beirut. In 1187 the city was taken by Salah al-Din (Saladin), then in 1197 by Franks again, who renovated the eighth-century Caliphate fortress on the city mound and added a moat to the south-west, separating it from the lower town. Crusader towers were built on islets off the coast opposite the harbour. In the late thirteenth century Beirut was taken on behalf of the Mamluks,[15] who demolished part of the fortress (further damaged by bombardments in 1840). The Mamluks built defences and Beirut became an important asset, supplying wood and iron to Damascus.[16]

Mamluk heritage is best seen in Tripoli but there are traces of this period in Beirut. The Al-Omari Mosque (beside St George Maronite Cathedral) is historically the most prestigious mosque in Beirut. It was originally a twelfth-century Romanesque Frankish church (St John the Baptist), known for its frescoes and converted into a mosque in the late thirteenth century,[17] when it was named after the Sunni Caliph Omar ibn al-Khattab, a companion to the Prophet Muhammad. The exterior and the interior of the mosque still retain some of its plain Romanesque characteristics. The inside is plain with banded stone decoration and carved pillars. In lieu of frescoes there is gilded calligraphic and other decoration on the ceiling, and elaborate chandeliers.

Another significant monument of this period is part of the *zawiya* of the Sufi scholar Ibn 'Arraq al Dimashqi, who had family links with Beirut and visited it several time for purposes of jihad against pirates threatening the coast and trade routes and for instruction in Sufism.[18] The *zawiya*, of which only a small domed chamber remains, was built in 1517. It stands in an area that was then outside the city walls and deliberately close to where the house and *zawiya* of Awzai had been. Ibn 'Arraq's *zawiya* was found while demolishing Souk al-Tawileh in 1992. The original would have most probably formed part of a complex with a courtyard and outlying cells and included Ibn 'Arraq's house. Before its twentieth-century reincarnation the *zawiya* had been put to multiple uses: it became a mausoleum under the Ottomans, then a religious school and in the early twentieth century was subdivided into shops.[19]

The *zawiya* of Ibn 'Arraq (Beatrice Teissier)

The discovery of this modest structure unleashed a war of claims and counter-claims from the Muslim community. It was first claimed as a holy and miraculous site by a Hezbollah-affiliated group on the grounds that it was the mausoleum of Ibn 'Arraq, an Iraqi Shia and Damascene. It was draped in banners and pictures of Ayatollah Khomeini and Ali Khamenei and visited by people seeking blessings. The Faculty of Legal Islamic Studies in Beirut argued that the *zawiya* was that of the Sunni jurist Shaykh al-Islam.[20] The dispute came to an end in 1992 and the building came under the control of the General Directorate of the *waqf* (endowment) of Dar al-Fatwa.[21] It was also acknowledged that the tomb within the *zawiya* belonged to the late Ottoman Shaykh Abd al-Ghani, director of the *zawiya* when it had turned into a religious school.[22]

## Early Ottoman Period

After the defeat of the Mamluks by the Ottomans in 1516-17, the Syrian provinces of Aleppo, Damascus, Tripoli and Sidon (not yet Beirut) occupied a privileged place in the Ottoman domains due to their command of trade routes and shipping. Mount Lebanon now emerged as significant in the next stage of Beirut's history. Mountainous areas of Lebanon such as the Shuf and Kisrawan (north-east of Beirut) and further north around Tripoli were dominated by powerful, rival clans: the Sayfa in Tripoli, the Assafs in Kisrawan and the Druze Ma'ans of the Shuf. The Tannukhs, traditional rulers of the Gharb,[23] were sidelined by the Ottomans because of their collusion with the Mamluks.[24]

The Ottomans' chief concern at the time was to receive tribute from these areas and as long as dues were paid, Mount Lebanon was left to its own political management and fiscal policy. Two mosques in Beirut reflect the changing balance of power of these times. The first is the late sixteenth-century mosque attributed to Mansur Assaf (or his son), Sunni Turkmen chiefs who had been confirmed rulers of Kisrawan after the Ottoman conquest. Mansur Assaf fell from grace in 1579, but power was subsequently restored to his son. The Emir Assaf Mosque is an attractive, proportionate limestone building with traditional Islamic detailing: banded stone decoration (*ablaq*) at the entrance and honeycombing at the windows. Re-used Roman columns support the central dome. The second mosque, built in 1620, is that of Emir Mounzer (or Munzer) ibn Suleiman al-Tanoukhi, a descendant of the rulers of the Gharb, who was Governor of Beirut from 1616 to 1633. His mosque (off Riad al Solh Street) appears like a fortified structure, with high walls and crenellations. The interior has beautifully plain sandstone walls, a vaulted ceiling and Roman columns, elaborate chandeliers and a grand marble *minbar* or pulpit beside a *mihrab* (semicircular niche that indicates the direction of the Kaaba in Mecca and the direction in which Muslims should pray) with *ablaq* and *muqarnas* decoration.

## Fakhr-al Din II

It was the Druze Ma'ans under Fakhr al-Din II (1572-1635) who proved to be particularly significant for Beirut. Emir Fakhr al-Din managed to expand his territorial control while playing a double game of revolt and conciliation with the Ottomans so as to obtain local governorships. He successfully gained Beirut (then attached to the province of Damascus), part of the coastal plain, Kisrawan (north-east of Beirut), the Beqaa and Sidon. At the height of his powers his domain extended from Adana in Cilicia to Acre, stopping short of Jerusalem.[25] A contemporary, the traveller George Sandys, described him in 1610: 'this Emer, he was never known to pray ... [he is] small of stature, but great in courage and achievements: about the age of forty; subtil as a foxe, and not a little enclining to the Tyrant. To his town he hath added a kingly Signorie: what by his sword and what by his stratagems.'[26] Much more unusual for a Druze leader of the time, however, were his dealings with the Medici court in Florence. The Medici, long wanting a share in the Levant trade, and seeing the waning power of the Ottomans, had on the advice of an envoy made overtures to Fakhr al-Din as a possible ally in the region. He responded by increasing contacts and agreeing to a possible joint military action against the Ottomans, offering his castles at Niha and Shaqif (Beaufort) and boasting that he could take Jerusalem. He even presented himself as a descendant of the Crusaders.[27] He also made demands, including sanctuary if ever he should need it. In the event, in view of a major expeditionary force mounted by a new Grand Vizier in Constantinople and the Governor of Damascus against him,[28] Fakhr al-Din fled to Tuscany in 1613. After two years at the Medici court and time spent in Sicily and Naples, he returned with no perceptible achievements, except a desire to emulate the self-sufficiency and skills in medicine, horticulture and gardening he had witnessed in Tuscany, and a taste for art. He brought back architects, a doctor, farmers and bakers.[29] By the 1630s his luck had begun to change: there were revolts in his territories and civil war broke out. The Ottomans had him captured and sent to Constantinople, where he was killed with all but one of his sons in 1635.[30]

Beirut was Fakhr al-Din's winter residence and he is recorded as having sponsored many works here: he built a palace under the direction of the Italian architects Francesco Cioli and Francesco Fagri,[31] created gardens and most probably added to the pine forest. Regrettably, only written sources attest to the grandeur of the palace. The clergyman and academic Henry Maundrell describes visiting the abandoned, but highly ambitious, palace in 1697: '[it] stands at the north-east part of the city. At the entrance ... is a marble fountain, of greater beauty than is usually seen in Turkey. The palace within consists of ... courts, all now run ... to ruin; or ... perhaps never finished.' He continues to describe the stables, yards for horses and dens for wild animals (a type of zoo) 'that would not be unworthy of the quality of a prince of Christendom ... to which they seem to have been desin'd by their first contriver'. The best sight of the palace, however, he continues 'is the orange garden ... a large quadrangular plat of ground, divided into sixteen lesser squares, four in a row, with walks in between. The walks are shaded with orange trees ... one cannot imagine any thing more perfect of this kind.' Terraced walks with orange trees rising one above the other led to booths and summer houses. Maundrell attributes, rightly, the landscaping of the garden to Italian influence.[32] Nothing remains of the palace today, which would have stood between the city walls and parts of the Burj, north-east of St George Cathedral. One tower (Burj al-Kashef) belonging to the palace and possibly recycled from an earlier structure stood until the mid-nineteenth century.[33]

The role of Fakhr al-Din in the history of Lebanese nationalist thought is briefly discussed in Chapter 11, but whether idealized or not,[34] it is disappointing that nothing commemorates his contribution to Beirut except a street name.

All monuments damaged by the explosion are under reconstruction and in the autumn of 2021 were not accessible to the public.

## Back to the twentieth-first century: Muhammad al-Amin Mosque

Today the skyline of central Beirut is dominated by this massively disproportionate mosque, ex-Prime Minister Rafik

Hariri's statement of Sunni power and personal vanity. The mosque was built on slowly acquired land (including a *zawiya* and souks) and financed by the Hariris and donations. Its foundations were laid in 2002, and the mosque inaugurated in 2008. Both the style and scale of the mosque, the largest in Lebanon, were deliberate and supported by the Mufti of Beirut, Mohammed Rashid Qabbani. A more modest design by Rasam Badram, which would have been in keeping with Lebanese mosque architecture and not dwarfed the Maronite Cathedral next door, was rejected.[35] The present structure, like a neo-Ottoman bully hogging the church playground, was supposedly inspired by the nineteenth-century Muhammad Ali Mosque in Cairo (itself inspired by the great Ottoman architect, Sinan). This is not to say that great care was not taken in the mosque's construction and fittings, under the Prime Minister's supervision (he personally chose the hue of the domes' blue tiles, for example). The site was awkward, and the mosque is built in two superimposed shapes (a rectangle, with an upper polygon supporting the four minarets) so as to accommodate orientation towards Mecca.[36] The sheer scale of the mosque with its multiple doors, arcades and arched window units impedes a proper appreciation of its decorative details, such as the Koranic verses carved round the façades. The interior is lavish and from various sources: walnut wood, yellow Riyadh stone, Persian carpets, chandeliers from Turkey and Europe.[37]

Rafik Hariri, who was also a Saudi citizen, was assassinated in 2005, either by Hezbollah or the Syrians. He was immediately considered a martyr, and associated with those of 1916, on the grounds of self-sacrifice through the rejection of foreign interference (i.e. Syria at the time). A poster of 2006 by Antoine Bridi shows the Prime Minister rising like a phoenix clutching the Lebanese flag and staring heroically into the distance beside the Martyrs' Memorial, with a struggling martyr at his feet and the mosque in the background. The whole image is surrounded by candles.[38] This cult of sacrifice was propagated with slogans such as 'They feared you, so they killed you'.[39]

Hariri's memorial is adjacent to the mosque: it is a huge platform made of limestone blocks, with steps gradually leading to the top, where the Prime Minister's body lies, closest to the mosque. The bodyguards who died with him are on one side. The ensemble looks, and is intended to look, like a dramatic stage: the plain, sober design characteristic of Marc Barrani's architectural firm. This is not the only memorial to Rafik Hariri: outside the Grand Serail is an angled, triangular memorial consisting of descending narrow pools of water lined with stone and basalt, with Jacaranda trees to one side (Vladimir Djurovic landscape architects). Another, consisting of three elements - a statue, a bronze torch and a rectangular metal pillar - is on the site where the actual bomb went off, close to the St George Hotel.

Another memorial in central Beirut that should not be overlooked is that of the highly gifted journalist and university professor Samir Kassir (1960-2005), assassinated for his anti-Syrian stance. This meditative space (off Weygand Street, east of Foch), which consists of two ficus trees beside a pool, provides welcome modesty, shade and rest.

## The souks

Like most of Beirut the souks, both in the present area north-east of Nejmeh Square and those that used to be in the centre of town proper, have had a long history. The present souks, opened in 2009, are in an area that was long occupied by shops and industries from the Phoenician to the end of the medieval period, when they were moved to within the city walls and the area given over to mulberry plantations.[40] In the autumn of 2021 the souk district was accessible, despite shuttered windows, with stores and businesses opening at 10 a.m.

The nineteenth century saw a revival of the site as the city expanded and the port and wharves developed. Key to this renewal were the establishment of *khans* from 1850 to 1870, of which Khan Antun Bey (with its private dock) was the most famous. These *khans* were more than inns, and contained storage facilities, shipping agencies, postal and banking facilities. With the opening of the first branch of the Ottoman Bank on the premises of Khan Antun Bey in 1856, the area turned into a business and commercial hub.[41] Hotels for Europeans (the first in 1849, Hotel de l'Europe), the opening of the European style Orosdi-Back department store (1900) and a new branch of the Ottoman Bank (1905) confirmed the area's growing status.

By the 1870s the press began to be critical of the city souks in the area: Souk al-Fashka (Weygand Street), for example, was singled out for its crowds and threatening atmosphere of aggression.[42] In 1884 it was decided that streets should be widened, despite protests, and foreshadowing Solidère's tactics of expropriation and demolition, old souks were razed and the process of creating the main thoroughfares of today (Allenby, Foch, Maarad) began. Modernized souks in streets perpendicular to the wharves and to Souk al-Fashka were created: Souk al-Jamil, paved in 1894 and Souk al-Tawileh. They became showcases, characterized by decorated signs, display windows and specialized goods. Souk-al Jamil, for instance, sold only European goods. A photo of 1910 shows neat rows of arcaded shops with shutters, gas lighting, signs in French (Magasin Oriental, André Terzis et Fils - see Tarazi in Sursock, pp. 228-230),[43] but with a few craftsmen still working outside their shops in the traditional way.

The nature of a number of souks in Beirut had already begun to change in the late nineteenth century, however: they dealt with imported and luxury goods and became sites of consumption for the rich and middle classes rather than of production as they had been. Shopping became a fashionable leisure activity, and the taste for European goods dominated luxury consumption. 'Made in Paris' became a catchphrase, often abused by local manufacturers. Other decorative goods of dubious authenticity and loosely termed 'oriental' also became fashionable.[44] Similar changes were afoot in the intra-mural souks as well. Part of the city in the later nineteenth and early twentieth centuries was still a maze of narrow dirt streets widening into more open spaces, and souks were positioned organically in residential corners or at the town gates.[45] Each had its own character.[46] The souk behind the Great Mosque (Al-Omari) for example, has a varied display of jugs, baskets, household goods, scarves and prayer beads for sale as well as vegetables, all under makeshift awnings.[47] Refreshments such as tea or coffee would have been available from street vendors. There was a thriving vegetable and herb market close to St George's Cathedral, with overflowing bags and baskets of produce and vendors and buyers carrying huge panniers, with local and European customers eyeing the goods.[48] As the centre expanded and streets were widened, prominent merchant families, such as the Sursocks (see Sursock, p. 223), established their own souks.[49] The wooden souk of Assour Square (Riad al Solh) was replaced by a brick one in 1916.[50] This diversity gradually vanished with modernization and the seizure of space.

The modern, post-civil war souks are a far cry from the originals, whether Ottoman, Mandate or post-Mandate up to the 1970s. Severe damage during the war gave Solidère the opportunity to raze what was left of the old souk area (some of them could have been salvaged).[51] The new ones boast that they lie on part of the Phoenician town's expanded grid (see below), and still have some of their pre-war names such as Souk al-Tawileh). This weak attempt at historical appropriation has not made the souks personable: they are big lifeless spaces, shopping malls, filled with foreign brands (known to all) and too expensive for many Beirutis and European tourists but not glamorous enough for Gulf visitors. On many days the shops (2019) attended by bored young people, were empty of customers as were many of the cafés in the area, where the price of coffee is triple that elsewhere in central Beirut. They are the antithesis of what a souk has traditionally been: they seem artificial and predictable in their retailing, with no sense of unique discovery (or of bargain) and even the small flower market seems manicured. There is no desire to linger.

A deep nostalgia for the old souks, their atmosphere, their variety, their different architecture and wide-ranging customers, has been,[52] and still is, expressed by those who remember them. A 1997 field survey to ascertain (from a variety of age groups) the memory of pre-war Beirut and ideas of reconstruction, showed that of the souks, Souk al-Tawileh in particular had been considered a significant landmark and its loss mourned.[53]

The present souks have nevertheless attracted attention because of their architecture: rectangular and multi-levelled, with herringboned patterned stone-clad exteriors, graceful high arcaded interiors letting in a play of light and shade and polished stone floors, they are a showcase for the architects Rafael Moneo, Samir Khairallah, Kevin Dash and Rafic Khoury.

In the autumn of 2021, the area was unusually quiet. Normally this area fills up at night and at weekends with people enjoying the restaurants in Ajami Square or puzzling over the luridly illuminated façade of the early Mandate period building known as L'Orient (after the newspaper, still going today). This shell of a building was not restored due to structural difficulties and is privately owned: it bears the marks of the civil war and has been empty since. Now only the propped-up façade remains, as

An avenue within the contemporary souks, shuttered in 2021
(Beatrice Teissier)

work has begun to modernize the back. It remains one of the sights of central Beirut that is genuinely pre-war. The building stands on Trablus Street, which used to be the main west-east commercial through road (to Tripoli), in a prime location. The building was originally bought by the Asseilly brothers as offices for their spinning factory; floors were then leased to the *L'Orient* newspaper and the Bank of Syria.[54] *L'Orient* was the first French newspaper in Beirut, founded by Georges Naccache and Gabriel Khabbaz in 1924. Both were Jesuit-educated and the newspaper was pro-Mandate, but eventually distanced itself from the vogue of militaristic, French Catholic patriotism and nationalism. It moved to the left, while maintaining its Francophile stance mixed with dissent.[55] The newspaper offices moved to Hamra in 1971, when the paper merged with *Le Jour*. Adjacent to this historic building is a bulbous structure dubbed the 'Fishnet', an as yet unfinished and partly burnt probable future shopping mall, by Zaha Hadid.

1   Jones Hall 2004, 173.
2   ibid, 172-173.
3   The Late Antique theological debates circulating at the time in Syria and Constantinople revolved around the single or dual human and divine nature of Christ and his relationship with God the Father.
4   Jones Hall 2004, 161-165, 196-201.
5   Badre 2016, 72-97.
6   i.e. the Ummayads, ruling from Damascus, established an empire that at its height stretched from Andalucia to Ferghana in Central Asia. They were defeated by the Abbasids. The Abbasids (750-1258) ruled a reduced empire from Baghdad. The Fatimids, originally from north Africa, later ruled from Cairo (909-1171).
7   Mikati 2013, 108. I am indebted to Hans Curvers for this reference.
8   ibid, 149.
9   ibid, 132, 152.
10  ibid, 153-154.
11  ibid, 239.
12  ibid, 222-226.
13  ibid, 278-290.
14  ibid, 100.

15 The Mamluks (1250-1517) ruled from Cairo and their hegemony spanned Egypt, the Levant and the Hejaz. They were originally slave soldiers of Turkic, Circassian and Georgian blood, who became a trusted military corps of the Caliphate. They defeated the Mongols in Palestine, took back Syria, and assumed power in Egypt under Baybars in 1260.
16 Eliseef 1960, 1137-1138.
17 Kassir 2011, 66.
18 al Harithy 2008, 219.
19 Ibid, 219-221.
20 ibid, 216-218.
21 ibid, 218.
22 ibid, 221.
23 The Tannukhs were a pre-Islamic Arab tribe which sporadically adopted Christianity and later Islam, settling in Lebanon in the ninth century, where they adapted to the Druze faith. They subsequently became rulers of the Gharb (Aley district, Mount Lebanon).
24 Kassir 2011, 65, 72.
25 Gorton 2014, 156.
26 ed. Gorton 2009, 82-83.
27 Gorton 2014, 55.
28 ibid, 68.
29 ibid, 154-155.
30 ibid, 167.
31 Kassir 2011, 74; Gorton 2014, 154.
32 Gorton 2015, 23-24.
33 Kassir 2011, 74.
34 ibid, 73.
35 Vloeberghs 2016, 222-225.
36 ibid, 196-197.
37 Vloeberghs 2016, 193-202.
38 Volk 2010 167-169.
39 ibid, 170.
40 Sader 1998, 34-36.
41 Kassir 2011, 135, 137; Hanssen 2005a, 217-218; Debbas 1986, 32, 34.
42 Hanssen 2005, 216-218.
43 Debbas 1986, 55; Kassir 2011, 225.
44 Abou-Hodeib 2017, 157-159, 171.
45 Debbas 1986, 50.
46 Kassir 2011, 434-436.
47 Debbas 1986, 51.
48 ibid, 61.
49 Serail Street, Khalaf 2006, 59.
50 Debbas 1986, 92.
51 Kassir 2011, 537.
52 ibid, 434.
53 Saliba 1997, 335-337.
54 Chognot 2010.
55 Kassir 2011, 498.

# 10. ANTIQUITY AND THE BULLDOZER 'MEMORYCIDE'

WHAT DOES THE CENTRE TELL us about Beirut's antiquity? Visitors who follow Solidère's heritage trail, whether going clockwise from Bab Idriss (Arab Centre for Architecture Tour) or from the ancient *tell* area and site of proposed museum,[1] will be brought (following the ACA tour) to the Phoenico-Persian quarter, the closed off *tell*, possibly the glacis to the north of Martyrs' Square, the Garden of Forgiveness and the Roman baths. These are accompanied by explanatory panels that in 2019 were yet to receive their text, apparently ready to be put up, but delayed or suspended because of the tortuous relations between Solidère and the Directorate General of Antiquities (DGA). Even antiquity enthusiasts, in the absence of proper maps and information, and because of the paucity of remains, will be at a loss to comprehend what this mini-package tour says about the ancient history of Beirut and what significance these piecemeal fragments of heritage hold in the context of ancient Beirut. Others with no interest in Beirut's ancient history may forego the following, but a brief survey of what transpired with regards to archaeology in this area after the civil war and what city planners call 'heritage management' is required for those who do.

At the end of the civil war and prior to rebuilding, central Beirut became one of the largest urban sites in the world to be excavated.[2] There were numerous rescue excavations led by foreign and local teams: many papers (academic and general) alerted the scientific world to this opportunity to modify, expand and understand Beirut's history, and warned of the importance of preservation and the danger of destruction.[3] The sheer amount of material coupled with Solidère's development priorities, the passivity of politicians, infighting and lack of timely publications meant that much of Beirut's history was not only deliberately done away with but left unrecorded. It has been called 'Beirut's memorycide'.[4] In the 1990s there was also a need to turn the page on the recent war. Today the DGA's policy kills transparency by forbidding archaeologists to provide any information to the press[5] and has site-specific arrangements with developers. Thus any visitor who is not an expert must rely on the courage of activists, journalists and bloggers to flag up the DGA's and developers' abuses.

A policy addressing heritage can be contentious even in the most culturally homogeneous and tranquil of places, but in a city like Beirut with its mixture of fractious politics, sectarianism, indifference and desire to make money, it is a minefield where destruction was, and is, the simplest way out, and also an excuse not to properly address the problem. Solidère attempted to project Beirut as the 'ancient city of the future'. Economic growth was where Beirut's future lay; the past would not be forgotten but reduced to symbolic fragments. Archaeology as 'theme park' was how it was explained by one author.[6] The 'ancient city of the future' slogan was ridiculed by academics and activists from the start.

Another questionable concept concerning archaeological remains in Beirut city centre is the so called 'Garden of Forgiveness' (between Martyrs' and Nejmeh squares ): a space that contains archaeology from the Hellenistic, Roman, Late Antique and Caliphate periods.[7] The mingling of these remains and the proximity of multi-faith religious establishments around it were supposed to create a site of peace, forgiveness and recollection.[8] Instead people see an incomprehensible jumble of ruins and are bewildered.

A mêlée of ruins (Beatrice Teissier)

Beirut is a small city with far greater economic priorities it may be argued, why should it accommodate its past history? What does it matter if many of its citizens have a mountain of other worries, or may find the past irrelevant or even culturally offensive?  In theory, heritage is communal and significant to all, but this is not so. Each group, each person within a group, can see and feel differently. However, for those for whom the heritage of Beirut matters because it is part of its identity, its image in the past, present and future, this history cannot be denied, demolished, or reduced to a neatly parcelled out consumer experience. Such treatment is not only as an insult to the city and to many of its citizens, but will leave its mark on future appraisals of the city. The city cannot be punished for its own history. Visitors will make up their own mind, but indignation becomes understandable for some when Beirut's prestige at certain times of its history and its early beginnings are known.

## Middle Bronze Age

The archaeology of the south Levantine Middle Bronze Age (c. 1950-1500 BC), despite still fairly limited and poorly published evidence, shows a time of urban growth with the development of settlements at strategic locations for trade. It was also a time of wealth, as exemplified by sites such as Byblos (royal tombs) and Tell el-Burak (palace).[9] The strong regional characteristics of these sites point to a system of autonomous city states or mini city states.[10] The oldest urban settlement of Beirut was the *tell* dating from to the Early Bronze Age.[11] It was covered like so many ancient *tells* of the ancient Near East by a Muslim cemetery, and began to be demolished in the 1950s and 1960s, which resulted in the loss of most of the pre-Hellenistic remains. The rescue excavations of 1993, however, did reveal successive city walls from the Bronze Age as well as from later periods. The growth of the Middle Bronze Age town is revealed by the development of its fortifications from an original mud brick wall and glacis to a reinforced wall up to twelve metres tall with sandstone foundations reinforced with pillars and a monumental gate (two metres wide) with a bent axis (*en chicane*, a technique designed to delay direct attack).[12] Such fortifications could not have existed if Beirut had not been a substantial centre.

There would have been a palace or a ruler's residence and one or more temples. A large courtyard covered in plaster found by the harbour area was interpreted as being part of a temple, but was regrettably destroyed before it could be fully investigated.[13]

The original city was in the shape of an arc facing the sea, covering approximately two hectares. The wealth of the town was also demonstrated by a cache of luxury objects (faience figurines, alabaster vases, basalt tripods, miniature vessels, spearheads) with parallels at Byblos and Ugarit (present-day Syria). Coastal trade is indicated, and more broadly Levant and coastal Syrian trade at the time showed contacts with Egypt, Anatolia, Syria, Cyprus and the Aegean.[14] In the Late Bronze Age contacts with Cyprus and the Mycenaean world are indicated at Beirut. There is no evidence of hieroglyphic (as at Byblos, heavily influenced by Egypt) or cuneiform writing from Beirut from this time. The first mention of Beirut as Biruta ('wells') in texts comes from the fourteenth-fifteenth century BC cuneiform texts of Tell Amarna and Ugarit.[15]

These remains or part of them survive on the ancient *tell*, but in 2019 it was impossible to see them as they were concealed behind panels. Looking through the cracks, the site appeared like another *terrain vague* overgrown with weeds and there was no sign of activity even through excavations were supposedly ongoing. The enclosures were set on fire in 2020 and the excavations suspended. In the autumn of 2021 this abandoned space was open, overgrown and strewn with rubbish. It was shocking to see that this is what the origins of this great city have been reduced to in an Age of Indifference, as archaeologists might name it.

To the west of the *tell* are the hardly identifiable remains of a Crusader fort and later defensive structures with a few rescued Roman columns visible from the back of the commercial Opera Gallery on the land side of Charles Helou Avenue.

The *tell* site was to be incorporated in a projected Beirut City History Museum, designed by a team from Atelier Bruckner (Stuttgart) on behalf of Solidère, with the futuristic outer structure by Renzo Pieni. The project, which aimed 'to tell the story of Beirut in the context of the new building and in situ archaeological park' pictured as a glass structure with a modern airy interior overlooking the sea, was on hold in 2019, and by 2021 was halted in a row over funding for excavations and the architect's plans, with the Saudis set to pay for the museum only and not for any excavations, and the architects not wanting to amend their plans to fit the archaeology. One can only hope enough material survives for the museum (if it materializes) to do justice to the city's past.

## The Phoenician period

The terms Phoenicia and Phoenicians are a Greek construct, with no evidence that the peoples of coastal Levant collectively identified as such during the period in question (transitional Late Bronze Age-Iron Age III or the Persian-Achaemenid period, c. twelfth and eleventh centuries to third century BC), even though they shared certain cultural traits. The dating varies according to each site. In the Levantine context 'Phoenicia' refers to four different Iron Age coastal kingdoms: Arwad, Byblos, Sidon and Tyre.[16]

The harbour city of Beirut was not a kingdom in its own right but according to the Assyrian annals and coins found in Beirut, was under the sway of Sidon.[17] The settlement, which seems to have developed from Iron Age II to the Persian period or sixth-early third centuries BC, after a hiatus, consisted of a fortified citadel around two and a half by three hectares in area, a lower settlement which was expanded, quays and a harbour, which was also extended.[18] Very little of these remains can be seen today.

The harbour would have stretched between two rocky headlands, now filled up, (Foch and Allenby). One quay to the west was found to be twelves metres long in places. The area had shops and houses leading all the way to the harbour. Some have argued for the existence of a fifth-century dry dock area. This has been disputed, with objections that the trenches could not have been dry docks, but were parts of an unknown structure of unspecified date.[19] The matter was settled by the sanctioned demolition of the site by Venus Towers Development Company to make place for three skyscrapers and a garden behind the Monroe Hotel, with its access to the modern-day marina.

The city was important enough to warrant a complex fortification system, which consisted of a two-phased stone glacis (an angled defensive wall made of ashlars interspersed with rubble) with a ramp and a staircase leading up to a city gate. It was strengthened and had casemate storage facilities added to it during Iron Age III.[20] Much of this evidence was destroyed during the 1960s, with only part of the glacis (now hosting rubbish) surviving on the north side of Martyrs' Square. The expansion of the lower settlement towards the south-west coincided with the strengthening of the glacis and was motivated by fire in the upper city and the expansion of the harbour area. The new quarter (souk area) was organized in a grid pattern, with some cobbled streets, and had separate domestic and functional areas. Houses, however, were not uniform (although all single-storey) and were of different sizes, from three to up to ten rooms,[21] with *tannurs* (ovens) and storage facilities. They were constructed in the 'Phoenician' manner, with ashlars on corners.[22] The biggest house, adjacent to others with a *betyl* (sacred stone) next to lustration basins and water channels, is thought to have been a local temple.[23] Finds of female figurines, and a later statue of Venus on the side of the building, suggest it may have been dedicated to Astarte. There were also unexplained dog burials. A dedicatory Phoenician inscription and a *favissa* (underground treasury) with hundreds of female figurines with outstretched arms, and depictions on Roman coins show that a major temple dedicated to Astarte/Ashtart had existed in Beirut.[24]

Sources indicate the wealth of Phoenician kings and their merchants, and while not having the status of Tyre and Sidon, the findings from Beirut indicate a centre with substantial trade and industry. The heavily populated Levantine coast line at this period is known to have suffered famine at times and was not able to produce enough of its own stable foods, but there is evidence that local produce was grown and traded: grain, grapes (for wine), olive oil, fruits and legumes.[25] Private houses had large storage facilities stacked with amphorae and it has been suggested that the port of Beirut may have been a transit harbour for selling cereals from Syria and Palestine.[26] Commodities such as timber, resins, limestone and shells would have been exchanged (by sea and hinterland) for metals (copper, silver, tin, lead), stones (precious and for building: carnelian, lapis, serpentine, basalt, marble), hard woods, ivory, textiles and luxury items such as Attic ware. Trade was both long distance (Assyria, Egypt, the Israelite kingdoms, Cyprus, Attica, the Arabian Peninsula, the Mediterranean) and local.[27] In Beirut there is evidence of industry in textiles and of what made Phoenicia famous, a murex shell dying industry, painting (with Egyptian blue pigment), stonework, ceramics and possibly metalwork and glass.[28]

## Roman and Late Antique

Roman Beirut or Berytus (in Classical and Late Antique times) was famous. It passed from Hellenistic to Roman influence (after having briefly belonged to Cleopatra) in 64 BC when two soldier colonies were settled there. It remained a garrison town (within the province of Roman Phoenicia, whose capital was Tyre) until a hundred years after Augustus (27 BC–AD 14) but was embellished, under succeeding Roman rule, to culturally conform to the image of a Roman city and to be a showcase.[29] By the third century AD Beirut had become a centre of learning, which further enhanced its civic importance. In the fifth century it was declared a metropolis.[30] Written sources, inscriptions and coins attest to major temples (to Poseidon and Aphrodite), halls, porticoes, baths, a theatre and an amphitheatre, colonnaded streets, villas, markets, a hippodrome or circus arena. There was an aqueduct and a sewerage system. Agrippa I (d. 44 BC), for example, had not allowed 'either the beauty or the size [of his embellishments to Beirut] to suffer by stinting expense'. The city was adorned with statues and replicas of ancient sculptures.[31] A large archway decorated with columns and sculptures is reported in the reign of Elagabalus (AD 218-222). It is not clear whether the fragmentary group of columns (some rearranged) in the Garden of Forgiveness may be the remains of this monument (a four-gated *tetrapylon* placed at major intersections), marking a major intersection of the east-west, north-south axes of the town, and the same as described by the Persian traveller, poet and philosopher Nasir-i Khusrau in the eleventh century. By the mid-sixth century the law school had become internationally famous and the city had the reputation of being splendid.

Christianization had been slow in the Roman city and it not known to what extent the building of churches changed the topography of Beirut.[32] Accounts mention the major Anastasia and Theotokos churches, as well as the church and monastery of St Jude and two martyr's shrines.[33] Otherwise it had all the civic trappings of a prosperous, prestigious city: a basilica, a hippodrome, theatres, villas, markets and workshops.

The city had an undeniably favourable geographical location and its wealth derived from wide maritime trade (there are descriptions of rich cargoes in the port) in textiles (linen and silk, from Persia and locally produced) and local agricultural products such as oil, wine and grain. Crops grown included wheat, barley, oats, flax, cotton, hemp, vegetables, fruits and nuts. Wealth accrued from taxes on all these, from artisan production of items such as soap and from activities relating to the law school.[34] During the Severan dynasty (193-235

AD) the teaching of jurisprudence moved from Tyre to Beirut and the law school was established. Education in Latin, both in literature and jurisprudence, was a priority, but knowledge of Greek was also required for a proper education. As the law school gained in reputation, people travelled to Beirut to study, and many important jurists and commentators were educated there, including some who helped guide and formulate Justinian's law code.[35]

An earthquake and subsequent tidal wave in 551 AD devastated the 'jewel of Phoenicia': one Christian chronicler seemed to delight in his description of people rushing to grab treasures uncovered by the quake and then being engulfed by the waves.[36] There is a debate about how catastrophic the event was for Beirut (30,000 people are estimated to have died) particularly as parts of the city were rebuilt by Justinian, while others remained in ruins. But the city still functioned, albeit reduced,[37] and some of its Late Antique features remained into the eleventh century as reported by Nasir-i Khusrau. The quake, however, had not only damaged the fabric of the city, but also its prestige.

Updated plans[38] show Roman Beirut to occupy an area under much of today's central area. The town plan seems to have grown from its Hellenistic predecessor and the grid was not rigid. The cityscape was the product of centuries of growth, and its topography, both in the Classical and Late Antique period, is still being worked out. There were temples in the southern part of Nejmeh Square down to south of Riad al Solh Square, with a road (the Decumanus) running west-east between the temples to bath complexes above Saifi Village. There were more baths in the upper part of the square, and in the now visible 'Roman baths' open area between Riad al Solh and Capuchins. Immediately to the north-east of these was a theatre. A main north-south axis ran through the Garden of Forgiveness. The hippodrome or circus was to the south-west, in the Abu Jamil area, and there were more baths beyond the hippodrome. There were villas, artisanal areas and markets north-east of the theatre and further west above the hippodrome and baths, towards the coast, and a ring of cemeteries to the south and west fringes of the town (Bachoura, Damascus Road).

Texts of the period are not very helpful for the location of monuments. For example, a finely carved fragment of limestone found close to St George Greek Orthodox Cathedral is thought to refer to the 'laws of the Romans', suggesting an association in this area with the law school.[39] Texts also mention that the Church of Theotokos was used by students at the law school.[40]

Roman masonry, as had Hellenistic before it, has served many subsequent civilizations as building material in Beirut. But even with Khalifate, Ottoman and Mandate-period destruction, the obliteration by developers and town planners (Solidère in the centre) of this heritage, which has resulted in the Roman cityscape to be barely decipherable above ground, cannot be excused. None of the trappings of the famous city listed above, except partial baths, are visible, and no one (who is not a specialist) can visualize the importance of Roman and Late Antique Beirut from what is shown.

The fate of the hippodrome illustrates what happens even to landmark monuments of ancient Beirut. The hippodrome, near the synagogue in Wadi Abu Jamil, was first excavated in 1995. It uniquely showed several phases and continuous use from the first, wooden hippodrome of the Augustan period, followed three phases (of the later first, second and third centuries) when it was embellished and the track elevated. It remained in use until the earthquake of 551 after which it began to be used as a quarry. Exposed structures showed ranked seating, north walls, a *carceres* (starting point area) close to the theatre, and the central *spina* of the track.[41] Despite lobbying by archaeologists and the media, permission was given by the DGA and Ministry of Culture for most of these substantial and evocative remains to be destroyed and the site given over to developers. The remains west of the synagogue, part of Solidère's estate, were destined to be part of a landscape design (with information panels) which has been on hold for years. Remains east of the synagogue were to be integrated in the basement of the synagogue itself.[42] As the synagogue area is presently out of bounds it is difficult to verify what is actually happening on the ground.

The remains of Beirut's *tell* (Beatrice Teissier)

1   Saliba 2004.
2   Sader 1998, 26.
3   Sader 1998, 29; Sader 2001, 217-262.
4   Naccache 1998, 140-158.
5   Curvers and Stuart 2016, 17-18.
6   Saliba 2004, 55.
7   Curvers and Stuart 2016, 18.
8   Asseily in Curvers and Stuart 2016, 21.
9   Charaf 2018, 439, 442-445.
10  ibid, 437.
11  Sader 1998, 30.
12  Badre 1997, 28-30; Sader 1998, 30; Charaf 2018, 438.
13  Badre 2000.
14  Charaf 2018, 443-445.
15  Sader 1998, 32.
16  Sader 2019, 2, 313.
17  Elayi 2010, 164, 167.
18  Curvers and Stuart 2016, fig.2.
19  Hans Curvers, personal communication.
20  Sader 2019, 161.
21  ibid, 166-68.
22  ibid, 253-254.
23  ibid, 195-196; Elayi 2010, 166.
24  Elayi 2010, 166.
25  Sader 2019, 276-280.
26  Elayi 2010, 163.
27  Sader 2020, 255-258; Elayi 2010, 162-164.
28  Elayi 2010, 164.
29  Jones Hall 2008, 52.
30  Mikati and Perring 2006, 43.
31  Jones Hall 2008, 63.
32  ibid, 161-165, 183-185.
33  Mikati and Perrin 2006, 46.
34  Jones Hall 2008, 21-35.
35  ibid, 212-3.
36  ibid, 2008, 72.
37  Mikati and Perring 2006, 52.
38  Curvers and Stuart 2016, 6.
39  Jones Hall 2008, 212-3.
40  Mikati and Perring 2006, 46.
41  Curvers 2017, 148-163.
42  I am greatly indebted to Hans Curvers for this information, and much
    else that concerns the Roman archaeology of this section.

# SOUTH BEIRUT

# 11. MEMORY AND THE DEAD DAMASCUS ROAD

'C'EST LE COMMERCE DE DAMAS et le rendez-vous central des populations industrieuses de la montagne, qui font encore la puissance et l'avenir de Beyrouth,' wrote Gérard de Nerval in 1842 at the time of his travels in Egypt and Lebanon.[1] A proper transport route from Beirut to Damascus had certainly become a necessity with Beirut's growth in the early to mid-nineteenth century, and in 1857 a concession was given to Comte Edmond de Perthuis (the representative of the Messageries Maritimes) for such a carriageway. He set up a joint company to raise funds in Paris and Beirut and the twelve-metre-wide carriage road from Beirut to Damascus was opened in 1863. This road, together with the expanding port, propelled Beirut's commercial expansion at the time and helped pave the way for its new status as an Ottoman *vilayet* (province) in 1888. The building of the 112-kilometre road, which replaced age-old mountain tracks, was costly in all senses: animals and relay stations had to be maintained, there were floods, landslides and robberies. Yet trade convoys and stagecoaches soon proliferated.[2]

Today this four-lane highway is better known to some as the civil war demarcation line between (Christian) east and (Muslim) west Beirut and perhaps remembered through images showing the rampant vegetation that claimed this space at the time. Beirutis will also recall checkpoints and violence and more than anything the sense of a city breaking in two, and, for some, never recovering.[3]

The war curious will be happy to be escorted down the street by one of the many detailed audio walks available or by a specialist guide. The focus here will be on different aspects of the road's history which are not evident at first glance, as one is confronted by a miscellany of residential, official and war-damaged buildings, various businesses, old stone walls - the whole dominated on either side by relentless traffic. Yet this road gives much: from significant institutions to diverse burial sites and dug up treasures, from historic foundation myths to spectacular modern architecture, to a forest of umbrella ('stone') pines to memorials of the dead. But first, a word of caution to those who might want to walk the road southwards from the centre: in contrast to early travellers who rode the open road in pleasurable anticipation of reaching the pine forest and its amusements, present-day visitors must prepare themselves for a mostly disagreeable experience. Having survived toxic fumes and the hellish underpass of Fouad Chehab, where destitute men sit smoking or urinating in the corners of a small green patch, the experience changes for the better (until after the National Museum).

## Université de St Joseph

If choosing to walk south from the centre, you will pass (on the eastern side) one of the most significant institutions created in nineteenth-century Beirut: the Jesuit University of St Joseph, off Habib Pacha el-Saad Road, which gives its name to the immediate neighbourhood (Yasū'iyya or Jesuit). This was one of the many French congregational institutions set up in that century (the Sisters of Besançon, Sisters of Nazareth, Lazarists)[4] but by far the most influential. Long aware of Beirut's prospects and in the wake of the Druze massacre of Christians in the Chouf in 1860, the Jesuits (under Father Ambroise Monot) acquired, through widespread fundraising, a plot in Beirut. They relocated from their seminary in Ghazir (established in 1843), founding a college dedicated to St Joseph in 1875, which was to bring them into direct competition with the Syrain Protestant College. By 1881 the Collège de St Joseph had become a university, with a Faculty of Medicine and a teaching hospital (1885, Hôpital du Sacré Coeur) and eventually faculties of Law (where it saw itself as the successor of the Roman school of law of ancient Berytus) and Engineering (1913-19), with an intake from all communities.[5] The University's main area of influence, however, came from its Arabic studies launched in the 1890s, which evolved into a faculty in 1902, its Oriental library and, above all, its publications. The faculty (under Louis Cheikho) focused on the history, archaeology and geography of the Middle East and Semitic languages (Arabic, Hebrew, Syriac, Coptic, Ethiopic) while the Oriental library, which offered oriental manuscripts, specialist studies and travel narratives, became a centre of research.[6]

The printing press, the Imprimerie Catholique, predated the university in Beirut: one press had been established in Ghazir in 1853, and from the mid-1850s more presses were added, moving to Beirut in 1875.[7] From the 1860 to the 1880s the Imprimerie produced mostly educational books (grammars, lexicons) but by the end of the century until World War I, it had become the most important publishing house in the Ottoman Empire, offering French and Arabic titles on philosophy, poetry, history and language.[8] These included the seminal *La Syrie, précis historique* by Henri Lammens (1921). In 1889 the influential and scholarly journal *Al Mashreq* (The Orient) commenced publication: battling Ottoman publication rules, it heralded Catholicism against regional Protestantism but also covered archaeology, literature, science and history,[9] moulding its wide readership to its vision of Lebanon. In 1906 the University issued its academic journal (*Mélanges de la Faculté Orientale*, turning into *Mélanges de l'Université de St Joseph* after World War I.

It was from this heady mix of learning, research and historical focus that during the French Mandate, when USJ was the training ground for Lebanon's civil service, that 'Phoenicianism' came into force as an active, nationalist and separatist political movement.

## Phoenicianism

This movement had its precursors. The ancient Phoenicians were already making their mark in France by the investigations of the Phoenician alphabet by Jean-Jacques Barthélemy in the mid-eighteenth century. But catalysts for the ideology had been a surge of findings regarding the Phoenicians from the mid-nineteenth century onwards: the discovery of the sarcophagus of Eshmunazar II, King of Sidon, in 1855 (on behalf of the French Consul in Beirut, Antoine Péretié) and the official French commission of Ernest Renan's survey and exploration of Lebanon, published in 1864 as *Mission de Phénicie*. Here, major sites such as Byblos, Sidon, Tyre, south of Tyre, and to the north Amrit and Arwad, were surveyed and randomly excavated.[10] In his publication Renan portrays the Phoenicians as poor in the arts, but distinct and superior in spirit from other Semites, and to be singled out, together with the Maronites, from the Arab Muslims around them.[11] Thus ideology and archaeology came to be inextricably linked, with the destruction and looting of sites and collecting mania a shameful by-product.[12]

Phoenicianism, however, was not the sole domain of Francophones in its early stages: it played its part in the Nahda (see p. 85-88), as it would later for some Arab nationalists. In their quest for regional civilizational inspiration Nahda intellectuals recognized the role played by the Phoenicians; Tyre, for example, was 'the most famous city of the Phoenicians and the source of civilization of the ... world,' wrote Khalil

Khuri in 1860,[13] and the special link between the cities of Phoenicia and Lebanon had been made by Tannus al-Shidyaq in 1859.[14]

Under the Mandate, the Phoenician character of Lebanon's ancient coastal cities and Phoenician proficiencies such as enterprise, industry, skill in navigation, the spread of the alphabet and of metallurgy, became established tropes. The irony is that the terms Phoenicia and Phoenician themselves were not native to the Levant at the time when the different coastal states that shared aspects of this culture flourished, but were a Greek (and also foreign) designation.[15] The true proponents of the political ideologies of Lebanese identity, however, were Henri Lammens (1891-1937), Charles Corm (1894-1963) and Michel Chiha (1891-1954). In his *La Syrie, précis historique*, the Jesuit scholar Lammens describes Phoenicians as bringers of civilization and, in Lebanon, the first to open commercial routes to the interior.[16] His message was that the theme of unity, which he saw running through Syria's history, would suit federalism in Syria, but that Lebanon's history and traditions from coast to mountain was different and (from the Emirs of the Gharb to Fakhr al-Din, the Ma'ans and Chihabs) led naturally to autonomy. Besides, he argued, Beirut/Lebanon was the 'mind and brain' of Syria and far removed from the 'barely educated Alawites' of Syria.[17] The businessman, philanthropist and writer, Charles Corm, became the central figure around whom Lebanese identity was expressed.[18] At first, he advocated Syrian unity, that Lebanon was to be part of the formation of Greater Syria. Then, with Michel Chiha, he argued for a separate Lebanese identity in light of rising Arabo-Islamic movements and rivalry with the British.[19] These Francophone, anti-Arab nationalist ideas were expressed in the four editions of the journal *La Revue Phénicienne*, which came out in 1919, together with discussions on economics, politics and literature.

Asia, wrote Corm, is a 'shadow' which must not further darken the light of the 'Mountain' (to paraphrase Kaufman.[20]) In the poem 'La montagne inspirée' (1934) Corm invoked Phoenician gods and myths, mountain emirs and the beauty of nature, as well as specific locations such as the holy Kadisha valley, to exemplify Lebanon's unique glories. He linked Phoenicianism to Christianity.[21]

Today Corm is also remembered as having instigated the first skyscraper in Beirut, the modernist, reinforced concrete, New York-inspired white Corm House (1929, off Habib Pacha Street virtually opposite the Chayla Stadium), which, with no concessions to local styles, towered like an elongated ziggurat over the suburb of Achrafieh and its gardens at the time.[22] It is still a hugely impressive sight.

The modernist Corm House (Beatrice Teissier)

Arabic, in the meantime, was being institutionalized as the official language of the state, and the Arab Press, in what has been called the second Nahda, was prolific and often critical of the French High Commission, nationalists and various affiliations such as communists.[23] The lawyer, banker, politician and newspaper owner Michel Chiha, while one of the chief proponents of an independent Lebanon during the Mandate period, eventually allied himself with Muslim nationalists.[24] He went on to be one of the architects of the National Pact (1943),[25] whereby the basis for Lebanon's independence and multi-confessionalism were agreed, and norms were established that are still applied today. Thus by the late 1930s Phoenicianism had been hijacked by nationalists of all hues, and by the 1940s it had become part of an established national narrative, even though rejected by some Muslims, who saw it as an aspect of French colonialism, while others appropriated it to the Arab cause, or found a balance in-between.[26] Other Lebanese historians, such as Assad Rustum (1897-1965) and Fouad al-Bustani (1906-95) in contrast, focused on a national history whereby the Phoenicians were considered ancestors only, and that the real precursors of Lebanon's identity were the Ma'ans and Shihabs (clan chiefs of Mount Lebanon)[27] with the Druze Fakhr al-Din nominated the father of modern Lebanon because of his stand against the Ottomans. In his *Tarikh Lubnan* (History of Lebanon, 1938), Al-Boustani portrayed the Arabs in a poor light: he did not believe that Lebanon had an Arab identity and thus, like others discussed above, separated the history of Lebanon from that of Greater Syria.[28]

Phoenicianism *per se* is now irrelevant to identity discourses in Lebanon, although in the civil war it was an ideology that suited far-right Christian militias in their anti-Muslim rhetoric.[29] The idea of Phoenicia and of pre-Islamic Lebanon, however, is still extant in the displays of the National Museum of Beirut further down the road (and the reason for this digression, see below) and in the selection of some surviving archaeological remains in the centre of Beirut. It has always been a useful argument for the uniqueness of Lebanon.

Today, USJ remains one of the top universities of Beirut, with multiple campuses (three of which are on Damascus Street: Medical and Infirmary Sciences, Human Sciences and Innovation and Sports), which architecturally are a far cry from the original simple, seminary-like building. It has two modern museums, the Prehistory Museum and the MIM Minerals Museum. The former is based on the extensive collection made by the Fathers and researchers over their time in Lebanon and on older and recent archaeological excavations and surveys of Lebanon. The displays include human and animal bones and artefacts from the Stone Age to the Neolithic to the Early Bronze Age, but also show the early stages of agriculture in the region. In autumn 2021 it was preparing to re-open after the trauma of the port explosion.

The museum also plays an important role in charting the destruction of sites due to natural and man-made disasters.[30] The Oriental Manuscripts Library continues to be world-class. In addition, USJ has centres outside Beirut: at Zahle, Sidon and Tripoli.

### Cemeteries

Outside the city walls, within reasonable proximity of the centre but leading out of it, it was inevitable that Damascus Street would be the site of Roman and later cemeteries.[31] Two major Ottoman and later cemeteries line the street on the right to the east: the Evangelical Cemetery or Cimetière Evangélique de Beyrouth and the Jewish cemetery. The Evangelical Cemetery was established in 1867 (and renovated in 2017) to accommodate

German, Swiss, French and some Lebanese Protestants. A walk among the gravestones will give visitors a flavour of Beirut's early Protestant European presence and also of Lebanese notables such as Al-Boustani, but also highlights the presence of a little discussed Beiruti minority: French Protestants. Their presence is first attested in Lebanon among troops from World War I and at the start of the Mandate period. Having seen the work of other Protestant groups, notably the Americans, and feeling the need to counter not only the Anglophones, but also Catholics and laicism, they aspired to found church and educational establishments. Yet they not only had financial difficulties, but difficulties in finding premises and pastors.[32] After the German defeat, they controversially appropriated German assets: in 1928 the French Protestant College was opened in the premises of the House of Deaconesses (the early Protestant Deaconesses of Kaiserwerth, who had come to Beirut in the wake of the Druze massacres of 1860) on Georges-Picot Street.[33] The College proved to be one of the lasting, positive, French Protestant contributions to Beirut: open to girls and boys up to eleven with its director, Louise Wegmann, rejecting proselytizing. She preferred, in her own words to be 'enabling conscience rather than conversions'. The College attracted students of all confessions, including Jewish.[34] After the French left and Lebanon became independent, student numbers at the College continued to increase and, fusing with the Lycée Laique (1909), new premises were needed. The Deaconesses' building was sold, and a new building, in Muslim west Beirut at Qoreitem (Madame Curie Street) was built in 1956 with the support of Ecochard.[35] Now a partially stone-clad, airy building, the College's agenda of a Christian education by example continues. Worship, which used to take place in the presbytery of the Hospital of St Jean and at the old Collège,[36] where a chapel had been built, is now held at the National Evangelical Church of Beirut.

Another minority in Beirut were the Jews. Their presence in the region dates to antiquity. Under the Umayyads (seventh-eighth centuries) and Abbasid Arab dynasties (eighth-thirteenth centuries), they were chiefly in Tripoli and Sidon. In the mid-twelfth century others are recorded at Byblos/ Jbeil and Beirut, paying land and poll taxes, like Christians. An influx of Jews came after their expulsion from Andalucia in the late fifteenth century, when they settled mostly in the Chouf. There were subsequent influxes after various troubles in Damascus (1848), and after tension in the Chouf (1893), one group came to Beirut.[37] Migration from Ottoman cities also took place in the early twentieth century. The Jews of Lebanon remained a minority and were generally well integrated, with freedom of worship under the Ottomans. In Beirut they were more Europeanized (French- as well as Arabic-speaking) than elsewhere, moving away from the old city and forming their own quarter, Wadi Abu Jamil, in the late nineteenth century.[38] They worked as merchants and businessmen, in financial services and as clerks and craftsmen, and were linked to the Sursock and al-Tawileh clothes souks. Initially they had few institutions except schools, but these developed with the foundation of the first modern synagogue in the Étoile Square (1922) and the development of welfare services.[39] The Maghen Abraham synagogue in Wadi Abu Jamil was founded in 1926. It is unclear how many synagogues there used to be in Beirut, as a number were also in private premises, but estimates suggest that Maghen Abraham existed alongside seven others.[40]

Not all Jews in Lebanon participated in the early Zionist project, but this gained momentum during the 1930s under the leadership of Joseph Farhi and Moshe Kamhine. Links were forged with the right-wing, fascist-inspired Maronite party under Pierre Gemayel, and a triple Jewish-Maronite-Zionist alliance emerged in response to Arab revolts of the 1920s and 1930s in Palestine.[41] Some of the Jews of Lebanon may have been somewhat aloof as regards what was happening in Palestine, but Lebanon itself was to suffer the consequences, and the story that led to the Palestinian refugee crisis of 1948, which had such an impact on Lebanon, cannot be disregarded at this point.

At the end of World War I, Britain had been given the mandate for Palestine, which included the terms of the duplicitous Balfour Declaration of 1917, whereby Britain committed itself to the creation of a national home for the Jews in Palestine while ostensibly not prejudicing the rights of non-Jews.[42] From the 1920s onwards, as more Zionist Jews arrived in Palestine, bought land and started to develop the country for themselves, resentment and alarm grew among the Arab population, as did nationalism. Unrest followed and tension came to a head within and outside Jerusalem with the Arab revolt of 1936-39. Its aims were to stop Jewish immigration, ban land sales and establish an independent Arab government.[43] The British finally advocated the partition of Palestine into two states, which the Arabs rejected. The revolt was brutally and comprehensively crushed, and this is considered to be a major factor in the Palestinian failure to recover in the war for Palestine of 1947-48.[44] World War II brought a lull to the local conflict.[45] At the end of the war, however, most wanted the British out, not least the terrorist Zionist groups who were becoming increasingly violent. The British withdrew in 1947, and on 14 May 1948 a Jewish state was proclaimed by Ben Gurion.

The exile of thousands of Palestinians, two-thirds of the population, ensued as did their flooding into Lebanon. Palestine had been taken by conquest and several factors contributed to the Jewish victory, such as the divisions and rivalries of the Arab liberation army, the *laissez-faire* attitude of others (Lebanon, for example, did very little to counter the Jewish forces) and the collusion of Jordan with Israel,[46] but it was British hypocrisy, mismanagement and abdication of duty that triggered in this part of the world one of its most intractable problems and created one of the twentieth century's worst injustices.

Under the Mandate, Jews living in Lebanon had been constitutionally protected despite official anti-Zionism, but some emigrated when Lebanon came under Vichy control.[47] The exodus of Jews began in earnest after the formation of Israel in 1948, even though some chose to stay in Lebanon despite a growth of anti-Jewish feeling. More left during the Muslim-Christian civil war of 1958 and during the Arab-Israeli war of 1967, but their numbers increased during the 1975 civil war as Israel's hostilities in south Lebanon mounted with invasions of Lebanon in 1978 and 1982.[48] After this period there were hardly any Jews left in Lebanon. Today the Maghen Abraham synagogue is off limits. Although the cemetery was damaged during the civil war, it was eventually partially restored and is now open, and has a janitor. Unfortunately, it was subsequently damaged by floods in 2019.

Damascus Street was always busy: early photographs show carriages, doctors' surgeries and even a Masonic Lodge (1861-95), but it would be fair to say that from the later nineteenth century onwards it was institutionally dominated by USJ and its medical facilities in the vicinity. Beyond the cemeteries, to the east before the National Museum, is one of Beirut's great successes of modern architecture: the USJ Campus of Innovation and Sport. This spectacular building (by Youssef Tohme and 109 Architects), opened in 2011, dazzles by its scale and whiteness and gives the impression of being both fortress and sacred edifice. It is made up of huge, angled connected blocks over voids, with irregularly placed small, square and rectangular window openings. It has a monumental staircase leading up to a gathering space, with two towers to one side (connected by walkways); one of the towers has squares and oblongs of different sizes placed in a zigzag pattern, which lighten and animate the ensemble. These can be seen to be in the tradition of *mashrabiya* (traditional Arab wooden window screens), in contrast to the openings of the main buildings which are more reminiscent of snipers' outlooks. The whole feels light even though it is so massive. The interior of the building is monumental, restrained and concrete, and though enlivened by the play of light and shadow from the varied openings, may not be to everyone's taste, even if the students are very proud of it.

The campus holds another spectacular surprise, which might be considered the treasure of the institution: the MIM (Minerals Museum, named after the twenty-fourth letter of the Arabic alphabet, which stands for museum, mineral and metal), which houses the collection of the chemical engineer and collector, Salim Eddé. This state of the art museum, opened in 2003, houses thousands of minerals from all over the world (including radioactive ones) and manages to be highly scientific, educational and aesthetically satisfying; touch screens show the angles and properties of crystals, at what temperature they are formed, a globe that can be rotated to zoom into a mine, film screenings. The best minerals and gemstones are in single cases, individually lit, and their extraordinary forms and colours glow in the dark, literally revealing the earth's treasures. The museum also houses marine and bird fossils from Lebanon.[49] It is now open.

## National Museum

The next museum on this trajectory is the National Museum, and here you will find examples of Lebanon's rich archaeological heritage as well as a throw-back to the local Francophone agenda of the early twentieth century. The French administration in Greater Syria had created a service of Antiquity and Fine Arts

A monumental entrance to USJ's Campus of Innovation and Sport
(Beatrice Teissier)

and the museum in Beirut was conceived in an atmosphere of enthusiasm for pre-Islamic archaeology, as part of an agenda for the French authorities' vision of Lebanon. Islamic antiquities were to be showcased in Damascus.[50] The journal *Syria*, covering the archaeology of all periods of Greater Syria, was also launched at this time. Its agenda, spelled out in its first issue, was 'to develop in Syria a taste for the art and antiquities of the country, to allow the outside world to familiarize itself with Syrian art of all periods, and to be an uniting factor between French intellectuality and Syrian elites, allowing for fruitful collaboration.'[51] A provisional museum (room or rooms) was created in the House of the German Deaconesses in 1922.[52] A campaign, led by Jacques Tabet, was launched to raise funds for a National Museum, and the plot for the current museum was acquired in 1931. The museum opened in 1937. The influence of Henri Lammens was strong: both Jacques Tabet (among the first conservators, with Charles Virolleaud) and Maurice Chebab, curator from 1942-82 and eventually head of the Antiquities Service) had been his disciples.[53] Chebab had also excavated at Byblos, which broadened the 'Phoenician' perspective to engender interest in Lebanon's pre-Islamic art and archaeology. As mentioned above, interest in the Phoenicians and Lebanon's coastal sites had formally begun in the mid to late nineteenth century, which resulted in the formation of many private collections. The original core of the collection had been the private collection of the French officer Raymond Weil, which he offered to the state in 1926, as well as the coin collections of Henry Seyrig and Michel Chiha, and material from excavations. The collections also increased through acquisitions.[54]

The museum is very rich in material from the Bronze Age to the Byzantine periods. Monumental pieces (sarcophagi, statues) and mosaics from key sites such as Byblos, Sidon, Tyre, Eshmun and Baalbek are displayed on the ground and lower ground floors. A staircase, with the carved letters of the Phoenician alphabet above it, leads to the first floor and early period collections. Of these, the rich finds from the royal tombs, temples and residential areas of site of Byblos are arguably the most impressive and intriguing because of their strong Egyptian influence and eclecticism. Egyptian influence on the coastal sites of Lebanon, which was strong and long lasting[55] but never overwhelmed local character, speaks to coastal Levant's widespread maritime contacts from early on as well as to strong local cultures. This ancient Egyptian connection is evoked in the façade of the museum (by Selim Antoine Nahas and Pierre Leprince-Ringuet). Regrettably the site of Byblos was butchered when first comprehensively excavated,[56] and is now not obviously intelligible, yet it is worth a visit because of its antiquity and stunning location.

Small finds of the Islamic periods are shown in a few cases on the upper floor and do not give any real picture of Islamic art and culture here after the conquest. It seems that much material was disposed of in early excavations, was lost, or is left languishing without context in the stores. Islamic art in Lebanon was, and continues to be, the domain of private collectors, which is regrettable. The famous collection of Foreign Minister and businessman Henri Pharaon, for example, which included ceramics, metallurgy, carpets and jewellery, was partially acquired by Robert Moawad, who bought Pharaon's mansion (built 1891 in neo-Gothic/Islamic style) in 2006 and turned it into a museum (now closed).

There have been strident demands post-civil war to give 'equal prominence to Arabic and Muslim antiquities ... of Lebanon instead of restricting its displays to pre-Islamic pagan and Christian objects.'[57]

As discussed above, the notion of Lebanon's past being a common inheritance is not served by its institutions.[58]

Before the civil war the museum was an elite and cultural landmark, close to the amusements of the hippodrome and park (see below), but during the conflict it became a military landmark, at the intersection of the battling sides and one of the more volatile checkpoints of the Damascus line.[59] The museum was severely damaged and looted, but thanks to the efforts of Maurice Chebab and staff, most of its treasures were encased in concrete, buried and thus survived. The museum re-opened in 1993.

Hostile streets, checkpoints and their brutality and sometimes absurdity are predictably a feature in post war Lebanese and Arab literature on Beirut. They give a chilling sense of the city's fragmentation and dissolution, and what this area may have been like during the civil war. Protagonists are forced to give away all their belongings, including cars, in order to be let through; they face hostility, are interrogated and generally harassed, and can be kidnapped.[60] The protagonist from Rashid al-Daif's *Al Mustabidd* (The Tyrant) questions the validity of checkpoints as the city is flooded with arms and factions anyway, and as checkpoints multiply and confuse, the old sense of the city is lost and he starts to hallucinate.[61] Other aspects of checkpoints, such as the harassment or worse of women, which must have been significant, or, for example, the fun had by young boys who evaded checkpoints and crossed from one side to another for the hell of it (verbal communication from a shopkeeper in Hamra), or occasional acts of mercy, were very real. These are ghosts that no-one wants to see, but which nevertheless haunt the present in times of crisis. The blast from the port explosion was such a reminder: windows, doors, the security system, storerooms and offices of the museum were destroyed. Yet, with the help of French and other international aid the museum was up and running again by July 2021. It also has a beautiful new catalogue.

May and Tarek from the film *West Beirut* (Beatrice Teissier)

If heading back north from here you will eventually face a mural on the Noueri building by the artist Yazan Halwani showing a scene from the famous civil-war film *West Beirut* of two of its main protagonists and friends from opposite sides, the Christian May and Muslim Tarek. Sentimentality aside, the mural is also a reminder that Lebanon's post- war settlement along confessional lines blocks natural cohesion.[62]

## Beit Beirut

Best seen when approaching from the south, Beit Beirut is one of the more striking war memorials of Beirut. This dramatically damaged period building, also known as the Barakat or Yellow Building, at the corner of Independence and Damascus Streets, has had many incarnations. It has morphed from family home and rented apartments to snipers' den and defensive barrier to potential museum of Beirut to exhibition space, to heritage site and vacant space. The Yellow House was built in 1924, the ground and first floors by Yussuf Aftimos, and the third and fourth floors added by Fouad Kozah in 1934. With its double, amphitheatre-like upper galleries commanding spectacular open views, the building must have had great presence at the time, as it does now, perhaps even more so, riddled and pockmarked by war damage. During the war its location was crucial to militias.[63] The building is a survivor (its heirs wanted it destroyed), but due to the efforts of a number of architects, academics and intellectuals, it was bought by the municipality, leaving the central conundrum as to what it was to represent, open.[64] Much of its surviving interior, such as tiles, furniture and artefacts, which testified to the life of the building, was cleared in 2008, leaving the detritus of war, graffiti and structural changes such as carved out sniper look-outs, pierced and reinforced walls. The artist and writer Tamara Zantout visited the site in 2000 and noted a baby's shoe and blood on a small teddy bear[65] amongst the debris: reminders of death inflicted both ways. A decision was reached (2003) that the purpose of the building was to be a museum representing Beirut's social and urban history from the nineteenth to twentieth centuries (the civil war being part of it) over several floors, with additional temporary exhibitions.[66] Restoration began in 2009, and the building opened in 2016. One temporary show was the 2018 exhibition of contributors to a book on Beirut graffiti, street and other art *Drawing Lines* (2018) by the street artist and writer, Tamara Zantout, which explored the complexities of Lebanese identity. Regrettably this 'museum' is now more often closed than open.

## Hippodrome, Pine Residence

To the west of the museum is the twentieth-century Beirut Hippodrome (for the location of the Roman hippodrome see p. 176-177) and the Pine Residence (the French ambassador's residence): both very much part of *fin-de-siècle* and early twentieth-century Beirut.

Horse racing as a westernized leisure activity already existed in the south of the city at Bir Hassan[67] when Alfred Sursock, grasping the potential for more recreation for the affluent, obtained a concession from the municipality (under Azmy Bey) to develop a project which included a race track and a casino in part of the Beirut pine forest. The hippodrome opened in 1921: a photograph of 1923 shows a respectable, well-dressed crowd of men lining the hippodrome during a race, with dense pines in the distance.[68] The present hippodrome, with a few straggling pines in the background, still has a horse racing programme, is open for riding lessons and is a venue for events such as food or beer festivals. The adjacent two-storey, neo-Moorish building, La

Beit Beirut with refugees in the foreground (Beatrice Teissier)

Résidence des Pins, intended and designed as a casino (overseen by the architects Bahjat Abdel Nour and Aftimus among others) opened in 1920. World War I had taken over, however, and it is unclear whether the building ever served as a casino. It became a military hospital, then a military barracks, and under the French Mandate it was requisitioned and modified to become the seat of the High Commission.[69] The building with its large arcaded façade and a recessed pointed arch portal (reminiscent of an *iwan* or entrance to a vaulted hall) and arched windows with black and white stone facing, stood in the middle of pines and was the focus of high society at the time.[70] But its historic legacy was not to everyone's satisfaction: after Clemenceau endorsed the separation of Lebanon from Syria in 1919, it was from the Residence that General Gouraud (who had succeeded Georges Picot as High Commissioner) proclaimed the State of Greater Lebanon in 1920. This united the cities of the coast with Mount Lebanon and four Muslim provinces (Sidon, Jabal Amil, Wadi al Tayn and western Beqaa), against the wishes of their annexed inhabitants.[71] In Syria, the Mandate created four entities: Damascus, Aleppo and Alawite and Druze states. As with so many French and British decisions and compromises at the time, these measures were to store up trouble for the future.

After Lebanese independence the Residence became the French ambassador's seat and is inaccessible to the ordinary public.

### Badaro

To the east of the museum is the business (banking, law firms) and sophisticated residential district of Badaro named after the industrialist Habib Badaro, who set up his textile industry here. The walker might want to wander and appreciate clean, leafy streets, varied architecture (modern and 1950-1970s), hip restaurants and bars. Enclosed on four sides by roads and highways, it appears as its own island, and walking here, despite some traffic congestion, is pleasant. This was a comparatively late part of Beirut to be developed (post-World War I): space and vicinity to elite institutions and the forest made it a desirable spot. As surviving pines show, this was once part of the pine forest and explains the emphasis on greenery throughout the area, whether on streets or balconies. The area was predominantly Christian French (with some Druze) before the civil war, but in the 1960-1970s Christian Arabs from Aleppo also settled here.[72] It remains predominantly Christian, and is residential, but with a mixture of NGOS, schools, businesses, a gated military compound and entertainment venues. Activity in the cafés suggests that the economic crisis had not reached this part of Beirut by late 2021, yet many buildings now lie vacant, with modern developments halted. Sundays bring unexpected new life to the neighbourhood, with a farmers' market (St Sauveur College) and an influx of Ethiopians who attend mass in the Christian churches and set up street stalls.[73]

Enthusiasts of the history of modern architecture might want to seek out the austere concrete buildings characteristic of the 1950s and early 1960s. This was a period which succeeded the experimental modernist style of the 1930s and had a new objective, abandoning classical forms for plainness, rectangularity, height and volume. Leading architects of this period, a number of whom had trained abroad and were influenced by Le Corbusier, were Joseph Philippe Karam, Farid Trad, Antoine Tabet and George Rayes.[74] Badaro has a concentration of buildings by Karam (such as the Forest Building), in a cluster around Alam Street. Other architects of this period represented here are Ferdinand Dagher (the Selim Khoury building at the northern intersection of Badaro Street and Damascus Street) and Khalil Khoury (Ayoub building, off southern Alam) More recent additions of note are Badaro Living (by Raed Abillama, 2014): this attractive, staggered apartment building (off Kirwan Street), references Mandate and earlier features of Beiruti architecture with circular windows and cast-iron balconies. In contrast, Convivium VII (2012), off Museum Street, is a throwback to the clean lines of 1950s Le Corbusier-influenced architecture, with striking red sun shades echoing the 1962 Raouche apartments by Karam on the Corniche. Other buildings to note are the ziggurat-shaped Midori Badaro building (facing the hippodrome, by Paul Kaloustian), and Badaro 3696 (Jafar Tukan Architects), a white apartment block with projecting, grey-black sun shaded balconies.

The area had its share of Mandate-period houses but a number have been demolished (some 14 per cent remain)[75] to make space for high-rises. Of these, the most poignant was the destruction by the Kettaneh group of the Medawar building (built in 1934), which used to be the family home of the prize-winning and decorated Lebanese writer, Amin Maalouf. Despite campaigns to save the entire building, the then Minister of Culture approved the demolition, claiming that the building did not have any unique traditional features (despite a lower arcade, stairs leading to the first floor from the garden, Art Deco railings and mosaics, balconies with arched windows).[76] The façade has now been saved, flanked by apartment buildings.

Otherwise the *quartier* has several French religious and educational establishments: relevant to the French Protestantism discussed above, is the Collège Louise Wegmann (opposite Henri Chebab), established in 1965; otherwise there are the Catholic École des Soeurs Franciscaines; the Église du Sacré Coeur, a modern church with colourful stained glass and mosaics in the apse; and Notre Dame des Anges (Badaro Street), a plain structure softened by a mosaic showing the apparition of the Virgin Mary to a kneeling saint.

## Furn Ech Chebbak

Damascus Road does not, of course, stop at the city's boundary, but skirts Badaro and continues into the busy residential, small business and shopping neighbourhood of Furn Ech Chebbak. A multitude of shrines and other religious iconography immediately signals its Christian affiliation. This is a lively, popular budget shopping and restaurant venue for the whole area, and not to be missed. Here you will see remnants of old alleyways leading to courtyards and traditional houses with central bays of triple arched windows. Along the road and in the neighbourhood are miscellaneous early-late Mandate-period apartment blocks and 1950-1960s blocks, with geometrical shading on their balconies or façades.

Another way of accessing this area is by crossing from Badaro into Sami el Solh, and here it is worth finding the Lebanese Fine Arts Institute (2nd branch), which used to be Notre Dame des Douleurs, a retirement home built by Edmond Rosenheck, probably in the late 1930s, and gifted by the Chief of the Foreign Legion in Lebanon and Syria.[77] Today it is a busy university. Standing in a small park, the arcaded building has a grand entrance, long two-storey, balconied wings and a roof terrace. At the top of a staircase leading to the entrance is a sculpture representing tragedy and comedy by Bernard Hussoub. Inside, although somewhat decrepit, most of the floors are still covered in original Mandate-era multi-patterned tiles (see Appendix) and staircases have their original cast-iron balustrades. Outside the enclosure, walls have some of the students' artwork and graffiti which are worth viewing, including the memorable 'IMF: International Mother Fuckers'.

Not far from the intersection of Sami el Solh and Damascus Street, in a cul-de-sac off Karim Rahal, is a small, possibly pre-Mandate stone house, which used to have an outside staircase, now blocked off, leading up to an arcaded balcony. There are

A house with flats in a Furn Ech Chebbak courtyard (Beatrice Teissier)

the remains of an underground passage in the grounds. The house is nicely whitewashed and is inhabited.

There is another side to Badaro and this area, however, which is not usually uppermost in people's minds, but serves as a reminder of the tensions that persist in the city. The Old Saida Road, which branches off from Omar Beyhum and joins the area at the Tayoune roundabout, was another old demarcation line between the Christian areas of Furn Ech Chebbak and Ain el Rommane and predominantly Shia Muslim Ghobeiri. It was by the roundabout and in the surrounding residential areas that violence broke out on 14 October 2021, as armed (with machine guns and RPGs) members of Hezbollah and Amal marched in in support of a demonstration against Judge Tarek Bitar, who had summoned two Shia officials regarding the port explosion. A gun battle ensued with retaliation from the far-right Lebanese forces (led by the war criminal Samir Geaga). Snipers and rocket propelled grenades terrorized the neighbourhood as people ran for cover, crouched away from windows in their apartments or behind their cars. The battle lasted for hours and left seven people dead (all Shia) with over thirty injured. For those who remembered, this incident had the deadly taste of the civil war, and for the young it was an initiation into what can happen, not only in their country, but on their doorstep. The dead were congratulated and lauded as martyrs, and a day of mourning was declared after the conflict. Tension remained high afterwards: Nasrallah (the leader of Hezbollah) announced that he had 100,000 troops at his disposal, but later tempered his language. Within a few days, however, things had returned to normal, with people crossing these 'lines' for shopping,[78] but with locals once again having to replace their windows and contemplate pockmarked walls, doors and damaged cars.

**Horsch, cemeteries and memorials**

Approaching what remains of the Horsch or Pine Forest is not for the fainthearted and visitors might want to take a taxi if not in the immediate vicinity. Once part of a substantial whole, the old forest of slim stemmed umbrella pines (*Pinus Pinea*, native or long established) of Beirut has been a feature of travellers' accounts since the early twelfth century.[79] The forest is mentioned by the Arab geographer Idrisi when it extended over twelve 'milles',[80] and subsequently William of Tyre wrote of it as a source of wood for the siege of Beirut.[81] It is probable that the Druze Emir Fakhr al Din, who appreciated trees and gardens, replenished it. In nineteenth-century travel guides such as *Murray's Handbook*, excursions to the Pine Forest are recommended for its fashionable cafés, bandstand and promenading space.[82] The section of the Damascus Road leading to Hazmiyeh (to the south, outside the city boundaries) and the English-style garden built there by Rustum Pasha was described by the journalist and writer Gabriel Charmes in the 1880s as 'the Champs Elysées and the Bois de Boulogne of the city'.[83]

The forest has had a chequered and tumultuous history, though: it has been alternatively and simultaneously a site of felling and plunder, of occupation (including by the Israelis in 1982) and a sports and dumping ground. And it has been severely reduced, with parts appropriated for other uses such as recreation and cemeteries (see below). It has also been cut into by the Omar Beyhum Highway. Today what is left is a park rather than a forest. It is a pleasant recreational, family friendly space of well-tended pines, but also home to other species such as eucalyptus. It has neat, winding, sandy alleyways for walking and jogging, there are benches and neglected picnic spaces in the centre, a skateboarding area and recycling bins. It has a sense of space that is very rare for Beirut and despite security at the entrance, it has a relaxed feel: people sit on the ground, couples walk around, and film and television crews might be seen working there. It is has also become the dumping ground for Beirut's redundant Roman columns (a playground for children), which lie forlorn to one side, and among which there is a damaged altar. The park was refurbished after the civil war (2006), but only opened to the public in 2016.

The old pine forest had a mosque, built in 1899 by the Damascene Sunni Hassan al Halbuni for Arab Bedouins in the neighbourhood,[84] but it was demolished in the late 1960s. Those interested in modern mosque architecture will appreciate the Khashoggi Mosque on Avenue 22, best seen from the Snoubar skate park (on the west side of the forest). This mosque, designed by Assem Salam and funded by a Saudi businessman, was inaugurated in 1981. Its striking feature are the star-shaped concrete planes which replace the traditional dome and an outdoor space of pointed arched columns. The minaret is campanile-like and stone faced.

To the south-west of the Horsch and just within the limits of Beirut city boundary is a cluster of cemeteries that speak of Islamic martyrdom as well as world war casualties. Some of the former are living memorials, and will be of varied significance for visitors but of interest to anyone not familiar with (or invested in) the concept of martyrdom and memory, and particularly by the devotion it inspires. Visitors with no links to this tradition will also be reminded of the degree of Muslim sectarianism and the complexity of Lebanon's conflicts. The vast 'Martyr's' (Al-Shohadaa, Sunni) cemetery, adjacent to November 22 (Lebanese Independence day) Avenue, boasts historic martyrs from the civil war of 1958 (Hilmi Naji Afifi, Jamil Mohammed),[85] when some 3,000 Lebanese died in a conflict between Lebanese Nasserite Arabists and the pro-western forces of President Chamoun.[86] Sunni martyrs and victims of the city's numerous conflicts lie here, and Don McCullin's 1982 photograph of a grieving widow and elderly mother supported by men of the family leaving the cemetery viscerally depicts the tragedy of war.

Martyrdom is taken to shrine level in the Shia cemetery of Rawdat al-Shahidain or the Place of Two Martyrs, founded in the early 1970s, beyond the Chatila roundabout. Here the most important martyrs associated with the civil war and conflicts with Israel, such as Imad Mughniyah (one of the founders of Hezbollah), his son Jihad, and Hadi Nasrallah, are interred in an illuminated main hall. Graves are adorned with cardboard cut outs or large photographs, with plastic flowers and copies of the Koran. The hall has benches for family members to come and pay their respects.[87] This cemetery has the feel of being wealthy and 'in business'. In contrast, a sadness hangs over the Palestinian martyrs' cemetery (within the Chatila roundabout), despite its well-tended graves. A vast banner of Arafat celebrates the PLO leader and is a reminder of the controversial role played by the Palestinians in Lebanon in the early 1970s. But the cemetery also speaks to the very early struggles of the Palestinian people and later the multiple assassinations of their leaders and intellectuals by the Israelis.

Among the most significant graves is that of Amin el-Husseini (1897-1974), an educated Palestinian Arab and a controversial but passionate anti-Zionist Mufti of Jerusalem.[88] Another important is that of Ghassan Kanafani, an exile from Palestine in 1948, who, while an activist, sought resistance through his political writing, journalism and novels. His novels, set in Palestinian camps or territories, speak of displacement, the disjunction between Palestinian past and present, facing up to the realities of the Jewish state, and armed struggle. He was assassinated by the Israelis in 1972. Murals of him in the Palestinian territories show how far he is from being forgotten.

The Palestinian martyrs' cemetery (Beatrice Teissier)

The cemetery also has a memorial to the dead of the Tel al-Zataar refugee camp (opened by Yasser Arafat in 1977), killed after a siege and assault by Christian militias backed by Syria in 1975.

A reminder of broader conflicts are the sober and poignant world war cemeteries: the French military World War I cemetery is adjacent to the main Muslim cemetery off November 22 Avenue, with the Commonwealth, World Wars I and II cemetery opposite, across Jaloul Street. This has a separate section for Muslims and cremated Hindus.[89] There is a Polish cemetery adjacent to the French one, not for combatants, but refugees.

1   *Le Voyage en Orient*, ed. Berchet 1985, 753. 'It is the Damascus trade and Beirut's location as the principal gathering place of the industrious peoples of the mountains that still ensure its power and its future' (author's translation).
2   Kassir 2011, 116-117.
3   Hayek 2015, 67.
4   Kassir 2011, 179.
5   Lammens 1921, 14; Kassir 2011, 197-199.
6   Herzstein 2015, 250, 254-256.
7   ibid, 256-257.

8  Kassir 2011, 195-196; Herzstein 2015, 257-261.
9  Herztein 2015, 261-263.
10 Sader 2012, 59.
11 Renan 1864, 836-837.
12 Sader 2012, 60.
13 Hill 2020, 174.
14 Quinn 2018, 4.
15 In Lebanon Phoenicia is defined archaeologically and culturally as the
   territories of four transitional Late Bronze and Age Kingdoms: Arwad,
   Byblos, Sidon and Tyre, from the eleventh-twelfth centuries BC (Sader
   2020, 2, 313). See Centre.
16 Lammens 1921, 3.
17 ibid, 4-5, 265.
18 Kaufman 2014, 95.
19 Kassir 2011, 262; Kaufman 2014, 89ff.
20 Kaufman 2014, 91-92.
21 ibid, 144-153.
22 Debbas 1986, 165.
23 Kassir 2011, 329, 332-333.
24 ibid, 335.
25 The key points of the National Pact were that Lebanon should be
   Arab affiliated, but not part of Syria, that the President should be a
   Maronite, that the Prime Minister should be a Sunni, that the Speaker
   of the Parliament should be Shia, that the military Chief of Staff be a
   Druze. At the time, however, Christians were in the majority, but today
   the demographic balance has shifted towards Muslims.
26 Kaufman 2014, 129-131.
27 The Druze Ma'ans wielded considerable power in the seventeenth
   century, to be succeeded by Sunni Shihabs in the late eighteenth
   century.
28 Kaufman 2014, 117-119.
29 Quinn 2018,14-15.
30 Usj.edu.lb.
31 Stuart and Curver 2014, 17.
32 Eyrad and Krebs 2007, 79-80, 98.
33 ibid, 89-94.
34 ibid, 154-155.
35 ibid, 217-223.
36 ibid,184, 220.
37 Schulze 2009, 12-19.
38 ibid, 27, 37.
39 ibid, 27, 35-36.
40 ibid, 110.
41 ibid, 40-52.
42 Hardy 2018, 66.
43 ibid, 73.
44 Khalidi 2007, 29.

45 Hardy 2018, 77.
46 Schlaim 2007, 79-100.
47 Schulze 2009, 58.
48 ibid, 119-178.
49 Lyckberg 2013.
50 Kaufman 2014, 123.
51 Paraphrased from the French, Kaufman 2014, 123.
52 Sader 2012, 61.
53 Kaufman 2014, 124,182.
54 Sader 2012, 61.
55 Sader 2020, 211-213, Phoenician period.
56 Maurice Dunand, *Fouilles de Byblos* 1937ff., 6 vols. Paris, Paul Geuthner.
57 Tahan 2014, 141 quoting Mustafa Khalidi 1977.
58 Sader 2012, 63-64.
59 Hansses & Genberg 2001, 231.
60 Aghacy 2020, 54, 156.
61 ibid, 153, 156-7.
62 Raidy 23 October 2017 ginosblog.com.
63 Brones 2012, 140-142.
64 ibid, 144-145.
65 Zantout 2018, 93.
66 Brones 2012 152-155.
67 Kassir 2011, 217.
68 Debbas 1986, 157.
69 lb.ambafrance.org; Kassir 2011, 256.
70 Kassir 2011, 267.
71 Kassir 2011, 256; Harris 2012, 175.
72 Kassir 2011, 326.
73 Nahle 2021, 12,87.
74 Tabet 1998, 89-98.
75 Nahle 2021, 41.
76 Talty 2013.
77 My thanks to George Arbid for this information.
78 Mezher 2021, *passim*.
79 Mikesell 1969, p.9, n.10.
80 Jaubert 1824, vol. 5, 355. The size of one 'mille' here is uncertain, but may have been the equivalent of 1-2 metres.
81 ed. Gorton 2015, 15.
82 e.g. 1876, 443; *MacMillan's Guide* 1905, 118.
83 Kassir 2011, 216.
84 Debbas 1986, 156.
85 Volk 2010, 40; del Castillo 2000, 2.
86 Volk 2010, 78-81.
87 del Castillo 2000, 2.
88 Mattar 1988, *passim*.
89 Cwgc.org.

# EAST BEIRUT

# 12. CONSUMING PASSIONS GEMMAYZE TO KARANTINA

STEPPING INTO GOURAUD STREET FROM Martyrs' Square still brings an immense sense of relief to most visitors: the scale diminishes and seems very appropriate to Beirut, which was once a small city. The street is narrow, many of the buildings do not tower and there are fewer cars. The mellow colour of the sandstone buildings on either side of the road enhances the feeling of sudden relaxation, although the scars of the port explosion and begging Syrian mothers dotted here and there are a reminder of Beirut's realities.

Gemmayze is a Christian quarter (traditionally Greek Orthodox and Maronite): churches of various denominations and their schools are more evident along this street than elsewhere in Beirut, but they do not dominate despite a few boutiques selling religious trinkets and devotional material. At Christmas, Easter or on feast days, however, the street does not shy away from celebrating its Christianity.[1] There are foreign language bookshops, art galleries, various individual cafés, as well as the usual fast food and other stores. The mood is relaxed during the day with local citizens going about their business, and there is a sense of community. After the explosion it was the local people, not the state, who came to the rescue and started the cleaning up process. There is none of the student frenzy that surrounds AUB (or the mêlée of Hamra). At night, though, its bars come to life. It is home to writers, architects, film producers and people attracted by friendlier property prices. It is a creative space: you may find a film crew at work, a radio interview with a local artist or architect. Yet for businesses and those living there the explosion was ruinous: people and cars were crushed, façades were blown away and interiors shattered. People had to start again from scratch.

This is a neighbourhood which is proud of its heritage. It was less damaged (compared to the centre and west Beirut) by the civil war, and great efforts were made to preserve its architectural character.[2] Much of this heritage was devastated by the port explosion, but by the autumn of 2021 (despite shuttered shops, cracked windows, damaged doorways and the occasional pile of rubble) much excellent restoration work had been accomplished (all from NGOS or private funds) with some buildings looking better than before. The character of Gemmayze remains.

Once known as the Route de Tripoli and the Rue du Fleuve, the row of late Ottoman and Mandate-period houses, the old tram terminus, the electricity power station (eventually Électricité du Liban) and the terminus of the Beirut-Damascus railway line at Mar Mikhael (1895), testified to the expansion of the city eastwards from the centre from the second half of the nineteenth century onwards. The area was also known for its early Christian schools and medical establishments, such as the École des Soeurs de la Charité, the Franciscans' Hospice, the Societé de St Vincent de Paul and the Greek Orthodox École des Trois Docteurs (1835, originally by St George Cathedral). The École moved to the Route de Tripoli/Gouraud Street in 1862 to the premises of the old Hospital of St George. Here it acquired its name, after three saints who promoted learning: Jean Chrysostom, Basil the Great, Gregory the Theologian. It still exists at the corner of Boutros and Gouraud.[3] Meanwhile the old Hospital of St George, established in 1878, was the first private hospital and medical teaching facility of Beirut.[4] The new Hôpital St George, which was located to the south-east of Armenia Street, was largely destroyed by the port explosion.

The street acquired its present name in 1919, after General Gouraud, High Commissioner for Syria and Lebanon, who leased the Rayes mansion (formerly that of Elias Sursock) in today's Sursock district. Gouraud and Armenia, which follows on from it, had one of the best sequences of pre-high-rise housing in Beirut: from late nineteenth-century villas with traditional, red-tiled roofs and triple arched windows, to medium-sized town houses with Art Deco or Art Nouveau features introduced in the 1920s and 1930s, and narrower urban housing allowing for commercial premises at ground level. Large plots were available to be bought in the Rue du Fleuve, enabling houses of a similar style to be built. Some are showcases for the 1930s 'transitional' to modern style, facilitated by the use of concrete. These replaced the standard triple pointed arch with other arch shapes (rounded, segmented, horseshoe) but also moved towards more rectangular shapes, simple stucco exteriors, the *porte-fenêtre*, which eventually replaced the central bay in smaller façades. In the first modern phase, reinforced concrete allowed for covered terraces (central bays were projected backwards) and or verandahs for single use.[5] Concrete blocks and insignificant high rises have nevertheless infiltrated the area.

The visitor may be rewarded by spotting the houses in this area that show vertical development, with floors added at different periods. An art scene that seems unusually relevant has also resurfaced here. In *The Lives of Others* by Ghylan Safadi (Art on 56th, Youssef Hayek Street), the artist paints densely packed groups of colourful people on mostly dark backgrounds (mute but each with their own story to tell), interspersed with archetypal figures (the king, a Madonna, an angel, a Joker). This resonates with the universal, never-ending cycle of life, pain and dark humour keenly felt at this moment in places like Lebanon and Syria.

## Mar Mikhael

An area that suffered hugely from the explosion was Mar Mikhael, a bohemian quarter to the north-east of Gouraud and Armenia Streets.

A striking modern building of this quarter is the East Village tower by Jean-Marc Bonfils (2015). It remains unmissable. Due to the narrowness of the plot the building (which consist of apartments, two penthouses and a single-floor house) was built in a cluster of three elongated blocks, one of which projects into the street from a height. A single red balcony cantilevered from one of its façades, while a green wall made entirely of vegetation (said to have been inspired by the gardens of the Électricité du Liban building in the vicinity) covered one side of the building. The architect, tragically killed in the explosion, used dark stone and wood cladding to reference traditional materials, which together with the green wall, contributed to the building's success. The badly damaged façade is now being restored. Restoration and renovation and the re-opening of its famous bars have ensured that Mar Mikhael has kept its character.

The Électricité du Liban building (shortly after the junction of Pasteur with Gouraud) is a landmark of 1960s Beiruti architecture. After a design by Pierre Neema, this vast tower hides many innovations for its time. It appears to have been inspired by Brazilian modernist architecture, which took account of climatic conditions, fostering raised buildings and outside space. Here the tower, a rectangular building with a projecting central shaft and an insulated south side is raised on concrete porticos from which the outdoor space flows. The lower public lobby was through a sunken piazza leading to gardens (not open to the public).[6] In 2021 it looked forlorn, useless and abandoned, aptly mirroring the money guzzling public institution that has let down its citizens over many years. Always rationed and mysteriously dysfunctional, the

The Électricité du Liban building, with forecourt and rubble (Beatrice Teissier)

electricity supply was totally shut down for a couple of days in the autumn of 2021. It was later reinstated to two random hours a day. The city and its people would not survive without private generators, but these, as prices rocketed from one day to the next during the crisis, were also in danger of running out of fuel and were rationed. Thus owners of mini-markets, bars and small restaurants sit in darkness, with no refrigerators, and resort to candles or early closure.

A reminder of Mar Mikhael's semi-industrial past was the 1930s Brasserie du Levant (the oldest brewery in the Middle East), which was lying fallow and damaged after the civil war. The space was used for an art installation by the calligraphic artist Zepha (Haphez). He made a series of circles out of dense calligraphic lines, two outside, one inside and one on a wall.[7] One of the outside circles contained shards of broken glass and was surrounded by detritus. The circles symbolized stages of identity: from the confusion and partisanship of war and sectarianism to expanding understanding and a realization of unity and identity. The artist knew this art would not survive,[8] and indeed the building was torn down in 2017[9] to make space for a much-contested, projected Bernard Khoury extravaganza. The place is now a building site.

A further reminder of the utilitarian nature of this area in late Ottoman and Mandate times are the old railway station and railway tracks of the Beirut-Damascus line still visible in the northern part of Mar Mikhael (between Armenia and Charles Helou, off Ibrahim Pasha Street). The period station building itself was officially off limits in 2021, but access to other parts of the station is possible by creative walking from east of Ibrahim Pasha. A metal tunnel (belonging to an old restaurant) leads to a hugely atmospheric wooded area where tracks and wagons lie together with piled up tables and chairs from the abandoned restaurant. The defunct tracks continue in a curve southwards.

In 2021 the nearby Gallery Tanit (to the left of Armenia, between Nicholas Turk and Fouad Boutrous) was exhibiting new and original scenes from the graphic novels of Jorj A. Mhaya: *City Neighbouring Earth* (2016, 2017 and forthcoming). An opening quote from Jeremiah (4:23-26) 'I beheld ... the fruitful place was a wilderness, and all the cities thereof were broken down...' sets the scene for the protagonist of the first volume who wakes up in the wilderness and finds himself in a Beirut far from earth. The city is ruled by a megalomaniac Batman figure who owns both drug production and rehabilitation facilities and who controls gangs of feral addicts who pursue dogs and humans in the streets. The protagonist can no longer find his home and has several nightmarish adventures. After forty days of madness, he finds himself back in his usual city, and witnesses the erection of a giant statue of Batman, who 'gave back roots to the Cedar.' The black and white drawings evoke perfectly a spectral, forbidding Beirut. The author grew up during the civil war, but his work is as pertinent to the despair felt by many in today's Beirut as it is to that of the civil war.

Gouraud Street and Mar Mikhael now branch off to both edgier and more sophisticated areas: north to the old quarantine area of Karantina (near the port) and south to the patrician Sursock district. Gouraud Street then turns into Armenia and on to the Beirut River, which marks the city boundary.

## Sursock

One of the joys of Gouraud and Armenia Streets is their stone staircases leading south. Narrow or wide, they bring enchantment and a sense of discovery to walkers, who for a rare moment in present-day Beirut, feel that this is a space made for them. The widest set of stairs - the St Nicholas - is also used as an art venue. People hang out here. These stairs lead to a change in mood from the bustle of Gouraud to a more sedate, exclusive residential quarter and the domain of one of the patrician families of Beirut, the Sursocks, and of the Greek Orthodox Archbishopric.

The Sursocks were (and remain) one of the most important Greek Orthodox merchant families of Beirut, whose close connections to Ottoman administration and Egyptian royalty led them from being tax collectors and dragomans to banking and a position in high society. The foundation of the shipping firm Sursock and Bros. by Dimitri Sursock, shipping grain with the Lascandi firm in the 1850-1860s, marked a significant stepping-stone for the family.[10] The firm was taken over by six of his sons, who each became responsible for a different branch, and it is from this moment that the meteoric rise of the Sursocks began. Although one part of the family had been in Beirut since the early eighteenth century (having settled near Byblos in the previous century, with origins associated with Mersin, Anatolia), others were established in Alexandria, Cairo and Constantinople. They took advantage of the favourable trading privileges given to foreigners by the Ottomans ('capitulations') and responded to local and global opportunities such as giving credit to the Khedive of Egypt, profiting from the Crimean War and the building of the Suez Canal.[11] Their offices spread to Manchester and London. They acquired (from the Ottomans) large tracts of land and villages in Syria and Palestine and owned holdings in Mersin. Eventually they contributed to the demise of Palestine by selling land and villages in the Jezreel Valley to the Rothschilds (contracted 1912, sold 1929), enabling forced evacuations and Zionist settlements.[12]

During the second half of the nineteenth century the Sursocks established themselves in grand style on large plots of land that were still uninhabited on the hilly area of Achrafieh, which overlooked the port. This became their quarter and power base, whence they contributed to most of the city's subsequent development such as the Damascus Road project, the port, the Pine Forest casino and hippodrome, the Museum, the souks, the Place des Canons. The quarter, with a road named after the family, became a centre of high society in the pre-Mandate and Mandate periods, where they entertained dignitaries, businesspeople, politicians, academics and artists.[13]

The Sursocks continue to hold important positions in business, the arts and high society. They were not, moreover, the only prominent Greek merchant family to have residences or roads named after them here. For example, there was the Bustros family 'palace' (1863), now the Ministry of Foreign Affairs on Pharoun Street in Mar Mikhael.

The architecture of late Ottoman and early twentieth-century Beirut was hybrid, both in the private and public spheres (see Zokak el Blat), but was particularly flamboyant in the mansions of the wealthy, such as the Sursocks. There are seven Sursock residences in this area, and it will be possible to occasionally visit some of these private homes after damage from the explosion has been repaired.[14]

The oldest villa of this area was that of Nicolas Sursock (d. 1882), which hosted the Grand Duke Nicholas of Russia in 1872. Unfortunately torn down, the mansion is only known from drawings and photographs,[15] but the flat-roofed mansion with long double row of superimposed arcaded galleries and side towers which dominated the area (all the Sursock villas had, and some still have, stupendous views to the sea) was more in keeping with Zokak el Blat patrician homes than later Sursock ones. These mansions (*qasrs*) seem to vie for originality and difference while keeping key elements of the old villas, such as elaborate staircases, central bays and halls, references to Turkish, Andalucian, Venetian and European styles, and decorative features such as polychrome glass.[16] Patrician families had their preferred architects and craftsmen, both local and foreign:[17] Bahjat Abdel Nour seems to have been a Sursock favourite.

The imposing, three-storey Sursock *qasr* (c. 1870, built for Moussa Sursock), for example, with its high rounded corner towers, pointed roofs and overwhelmingly rectangular windows with stucco decoration above (hinting at arches), combines a semi-European aspect with traditional features such as a sweeping double staircase above a fountain, and an entrance superimposed by triple arches and balconies on either side.[18] In 2020 it was still the residence Lady Yvonne Sursock (née Cochrane) and family. The damage from the explosion to this *qasr* was extensive; parts of the roof collapsed, walls, doors and fittings were blown apart, windows shattered, furnishings and possessions pulverized. The elderly socialite and philanthropist Lady Sursock survived the explosion with some damage to her legs, but died from heart failure later in the month. Her family is convinced that the trauma of the explosion precipitated her death. In a moving interview, her son Roderick expressed his anger at 'the corrupt gang of people who run the country' whom he held responsible for the tragedy. He saw twenty years of restoration blown apart in an instant, in damage that was far worse than during the civil war. There seems to be no point in fully restoring the palace now, he continued, until Lebanon changes.[19] If and when restored, the plan seems to be to open the house as a museum.

The home of the art collector, Nicolas Sursock (1875-1952, son of Nicolas Sursock), built in 1912 and now the Museum Sursock, is strikingly different. Here the ensemble, with its brilliant white exterior, double curved staircase and horseshoe arches filled with a fretwork of polychrome glass, looks like an elaborate piece of lace work. It is particularly striking at night when lit from within. Other Sursock houses are not as sumptuous. For example, the house of Elias Sursock (built in the mid- to late 1800s) was demolished in the 1960s (over an inheritance dispute), was rebuilt and renovated, and is now known as the Maison Rayes as a smaller replica of the original. It features white marble arcades, parquet flooring, door handles, polychrome glass and marquetry made by Carlo Bugatti.[20] The *qasr* of Halil Sursock, built in the 1880s, has none of the flourish of the above: it is a plain and attractive mansion with a pitched red-tiled roof, rectangular windows, circular windows and a modest outside staircase with a wrought-iron balustrade. In keeping with other patrician houses elsewhere, this house has changed hands many times: it became a Mokbel family property, then a school in the 1960s, and was then the Pigier business school.[21] Another smaller Sursock villa (c. 1920s), which now belongs to the interior decorator May Daouk, has kept its modest exterior and some of its internal layout including the traditional central hall separated by a triple arch, with clear (as opposed to coloured) fretwork glass.[22]

Most of these buildings have undergone extensive renovations, but usually blended so as not to be too obvious. Now many have had to start the process all over again. The Nicolas Sursock home, left to the citizens of Lebanon as a museum, is a case in point. From 2008 to 2014 the mansion was refurbished as a museum: sky lights were added, underground spaces were made below the garden for an exhibition space, a library, a conservation workshop, a café and an auditorium. Inside, original features, such as the Salon Arabe with closed off oculi and tiles were kept. The refurbishment was worth it, as the legacy of this museum and present contribution to the cultural life of the city are immense. It has a permanent collection of archives, old photographs (including the Debbas photographic collection, so frequently referred to here) and artworks, but has also hosted a variety of temporary exhibitions and has a comprehensive research library on the history and art of Beirut. The museum itself and the collections suffered extensive damage during the explosion, but renovations are in progress, with some damaged works sent to the Pompidou Centre in Paris for restoration. It was partially reopened in July 2021 for film screenings, workshops and outdoor performances. It aims to fully reopen in the spring of 2022.

The interiors of these mansions have also had eclectic and peripatetic lives. Furnishings, added to by successive generations, show a taste for orientalist-style rooms with elements of neo-Gothic mixed with European. The orientalist look was created both by imports from eighteenth- and nineteenth-century Damascene and Aleppine palaces (whole ceilings including *muqarnas* and *mashrabiya* motifs, panelling, doors, furniture, decorative calligraphy) and decoration inspired by books such as *L'Art Arabe* by Emile Prisse d'Avennes (1877).[23] Catastrophically, the explosion caused not only extensive damage to exteriors, but to the interiors of these buildings, including to rare marquetry.

The major provider of furnishings from Syria was the firm Tarazi (and Terzis) et Fils, which understood the commercial value of tapping into the mid-nineteenth-century vogue for orientalism and the availability of material resulting from the destruction wrought by the 1860 massacre of Christians in Syria and subsequent house renovations. They became restorers, embellishers and designers. Damascus at the time was also famous for its silks, marquetry, decorated metal work, weaponry and glass. There was a hunger for all of the above but also for marble fountains, other stonework, carpets and even Bedouin robes. The Tarazi family itself moved to Beirut and Athens after 1860 but continued to have a relationship with various workshops in Damascus. In 1862, Dimitri Tarazi founded his first shop in Beirut. Then his younger brother André Tarazi (which became Terzis as the Greek name was transformed) came from Athens in 1868 to work with Dimitri until 1894. Their shop, Dimitri and André Tarazi, was in Khan el Touteh in the Souk el Bazerkan. After their separation in 1894, the Dimitri Tarazi & Fils shop was named Au Musée Oriental established in the new Souk el Gemil in Beirut, then with various branches opening in Jerusalem, Damascus, Cairo and Alexandria. Au Magasin Oriental then opened a branch in Jerusalem. By the 1880s they had established a presence in the Beiruti souk of el Bazerkan with goods (wood, copper, bronze) made in or procured from Damascus and elsewhere in Syria. Dimitri Tarazi & Fils also became suppliers to Sultan Abdul Hamid II and to European courts. Thus in Beirut they were responsible for the oriental and orientalizing furnishings (some made from drawings by Gebran Dimitri Tarazi)[24] in the private homes of wealthy notables, such as the Sursocks, the Maison Daouk or the Palais Pharaon. Some of these interiors can be traced back to their origins, such as parts of Aleppo's Ghazalé palace in Henry Pharaon's house, Damascene *boiseries* (panelling and other woodwork) in the Villa Sursock, and nineteenth-century wood in the Salon Arabe of the Sursock Museum. These boiseries would be renovated and sometimes embellished with gold work. Others, such as those in the Linda and Michel Sursock villa, were wholly designed by the firm.[25]

Maison Tarazi was also responsible for the decoration of early Mandate-era public buildings such the Casino 'Cercle du Parc', the Résidence des Pins and the Théâtre de Beirut. The acquisition of Syrian interiors and goods continued through the Mandate period and beyond.[26] In the 1960s a Petit Salon Oriental was created by the Tarazis in a pavilion in the grounds of the Sursock-Cochrane mansion. After major disruption during the civil war (there was a shop in the Hotel Alcazar until 1987 when it closed and operations moved to Broumana), Tarazi design and craft is in demand again and the workshop is now active, supplying private homes and other venues not only in Beirut but abroad (London, the Côte d'Azur, Mykonos, Amman, Jeddah, Riyad).[27] There was a Tarazi boutique on Pharaon Street, Mar Mikhael, which was blown apart by the explosion, but by the autumn of 2021 was whole again but empty of stock. Undefeated, Camille Tarazi's fifth-generation firm is championing the salvage and reconstruction of period interiors, in which his book *Vitrine de l'Orient* (2015) has proved invaluable as are the family archives.[28]

Sursock homes are also full of mementoes that go back generations and are hugely significant for the history of the family and of Beirut. But the sheer amount of material, whether family portraits, signed photographs of important people, historic documents, Flemish tapestries, Byzantine glass and other small antiquities, monumental vases, marble statues, crafted cabinets, personalized porcelain or art work by artists such as Guercino or Ribera, displayed in close proximity in a mixture of oriental, neo-Gothic and European decoration and furnishings, can end up, like all the collections of great houses, looking like surplus merchandise.

The proximity of these houses meant close family interaction and often access through gardens. The garden of the Sursock palace is the only one which retains a park-like quality.

Sursock Street's cachet is also defined by the Greek Orthodox Archbishopric, which, together with St George Cathedral in the centre, is a reminder of the significant presence of this community in Beirut. The community, once known as the Rum Orthodox, adheres to Antiochian Byzantine rite, and in Beirut has complex and longstanding (since antiquity and subsequently) migrant origins from the Middle East (Syria,

Asia Minor, Alexandretta) as well as from Greece and its islands, Russia and Palestine. It is now the second largest Christian denomination in Lebanon after the Maronites.

The Archbishopric, originally a handsome late nineteenth- or early twentieth-century traditional villa with long wings and a central staircase,[29] has been refurbished and embellished with a top heavy ornate pillared entrance. This space is heavily guarded and not open to the public.

## Mar Mitr cemetery

More accessible is the Greek Orthodox cemetery of Mar Mitr, to the south-east of Sursock Street adjacent to the Mar Mitr (St Demetrius) Church and immediately east of the Alfred Naccache freeway. The church of Mar Mitr was built on the site of previous sanctuaries (Roman sarcophagi have been found there) and a chapel. The present building has nineteenth-century origins, but is now a fresh looking, graceful, arcaded building with banded stone bell towers. The church, except for the iconostasis, was ruined by the explosion. It was restored with the help of the Moscow Patriarchate, and was due to re-open in 2021 on the feast of St Demetrius (26 October).

The cemetery was developed during the Egyptian occupation (1832-40) when it was stipulated that cemeteries should be *extra muros* for hygienic reasons.[30] This cemetery is the most important of those related to the Greek community and is particularly interesting for reflecting the tastes and social standing of the community through time. The first part, established from 1835-60, was the northern plot: it consisted of austere rectangular burial plots, made of sandstone blocks with no decoration. Many are anonymous. As time went by the style changed, tombstones had longer epitaphs, more decoration and epigraphic flourishes.[31] The central part of the cemetery became the domain of Cypriots, Greek minorities and Russians. The prime position, in front of the church and on the adjacent rise, began to be used in the last quarter of the nineteenth and early part of the twentieth centuries and became the wealthy patrician quarter occupied by the likes of the Sursock, Jbeily, Debbas, Bustros and Tarazi (or Terzis) families.[32] These tombs, of a *ciborium* type (columned canopies) on podia surrounded by plants, are imposing marble monuments embellished with elaborate Christian symbols of angels, doves and crosses and other motifs. One alley is devoted solely to the Sursocks, imprinting themselves in the geography of the cemetery in death much as they did in the city in life.[33]

The Eastern Orthodox Trad family tombs are to the north-west, and some have been refashioned to look monumental.[34] Other tombs of note are soberly aligned, gabled mausolea with plain doors and only a Byzantine cross for decoration and standardized calligraphy.[35] The eastern part of the cemetery began to be occupied from the 1940s onwards as did appropriation of the space by a wider range of society. Crowding began in earnest from the 1960s onwards, and this phenomenon is at its most depressing at the back of the church where tombs consist of simple, superimposed chambers in an airless, narrow alley-like space, barely allowing the visitor room, let alone time, for reflection. Many of the old tombs have been removed and refashioned, sometimes in the European style, using dark granite as opposed to marble. Concrete tombs are also now a feature of the cemetery.[36] The Tueni family also claims part of this cemetery, and a reminder of Beirut's problems is to be found in the tomb of the murdered anti-Syrian journalist and editor, Gebran Ghassan Tueni (1957-2005), marked by a portrait mosaic. His assassination followed that of his colleague Samir Kassir (see p. 159).

## Back to Gouraud

Walking from Gouraud Street into Armenia Street the mood becomes increasingly restless: roads rather than open stairways intersect the street, there is more traffic and it is busy with garages and small businesses. It feels rougher. Armenia Street, named after successive waves of Armenian settler refugees fleeing genocide, leads to the Beirut River and over the Charles Helou bridge to the predominantly Armenian municipality of Burj Hammud. Flowing from Mount Lebanon, the Beirut River, known as the Magoras in antiquity once serviced the city via a Roman aqueduct. Its banks here were turned into industrial and storage sites because of the river's proximity to the port, while its eastern edge also became an Armenian shanty town. The river itself, dry as a bone in summer, has been highly abused: polluted from an abattoir in the vicinity (now closed) and often serving as a rubbish dump.

Burj Hammud is outside the Beirut city limits, but parts of it are very accessible from here. The busy, friendly working-class character, including spoken language, signage, denominational feel and food, is very Armenian, but it now has a mixed working-class population of Muslim Arabs, Kurds and refugees.

## Karantina

Turning north from Armenia into Al Khoder Street, and then across Charles Helou, leads to Karantina: a space that encapsulates Beirut's tragedy but also its creativity. It is a dense, part Muslim, part Christian and migrant area, a mix of residential, industrial estate, commercial space (Beirut Forum), gallery space and club venue. The residential area, so close to the port, felt the brunt of the explosion. Port workers and other residents were literally thrown back by its shock waves as already worn down and war damaged buildings were blasted away from

Residents sitting outside a renovated building, with Jamaila taking a photo
(Beatrice Teissier)

them, with many inside. Help from volunteers and NGOs was at hand and vital as many residents who could not afford to move away moved to tents. Many were displaced elsewhere.[37] By October 2021 the area had returned to a semblance of quiet and normality with much repair and some renewal, with varying levels of adequacy, as reported by the inhabitants.

Nevertheless, the residential part of Karantina is still one of the few areas of Beirut that feels to scale and very human: there is a small park, children play in the street, people sit outside and chat, houses are small (some period) and apartment blocks do not loom over the streets. The fear is that such parts of Karantina will be swallowed up by some grand port regeneration scheme. Students and others are already working on 'adaptive strategies' for transforming the port area and Karantina.[38] To what extent would the locals want the area to be transformed? Priced out of their homes they would have to relocate once more.

Karantina refers the site of the old 'lazaretto' built here in the time of Ibrahim Pasha (the then Governor of Syria,1832-40) at the time the port was being enlarged and commercial steamships came into being. The place lent itself to the docking of ships and it became an obligatory port of call for ships in the eastern Mediterranean, and thus although its organization was chaotic at first, the lazaretto helped establish Beirut as a nodal port. The lazaretto later became a source of infection itself, from overcrowding and the presence of cholera and even plague. It became a shanty town, with Armenian refugees placed in a transit camp there before moving on to Burj Hammud. A fire destroyed the camp in 1933.[39]

The area went on to have a further, darker history. It became a refugee camp for Palestinians after 1948, a population which also included Kurds and Syrians. By the 1970s it was controlled by the PLO and in 1976 became the site of what is known as the Karantina massacre: some 2,000 people were killed and others displaced by the right-wing Christian Phalangist party. The irony and poignancy of the situation is shown in Don McCullin's 1976 photograph of two elderly Palestinian being escorted out of a burning Karantina by the very people who caused the massacre: the Phalangists. In the same year, the PLO, which had now joined the wider war, and the Lebanese National Movement retaliated with a (lesser) massacre in the Christian town of Damour, which was a stronghold of the Christian Phalange.[40]

An association with defiance and resistance continues in Karantina, with Sayed Hassam Nasrullah, the present leader of Hezbollah, claiming it as his birthplace.[41] Karantina has suffered in other ways: from the stench and detritus of an old abattoir, and like the Beirut River, from the rubbish dumped there on a vacant plot during the 2015 refuse crisis.[42]

The space and edginess of parts of Karantina, however, have been an inspiration to architects, a number of whom set up their practices there. The contrast between the residential and the dirty industrial area could not be greater. In reaction to the war and the scarred realities of Karantina, the architect Bernard Khoury designed the B018 nightclub (opened 1998, refurbished 2019). It was designed as an underground bunker, even mortuary space (some four metres below ground) decorated in black, where advertised 'sound rituals' bring to mind the defiant madness of Hades. A large circular iron plate around which is a circular parking lot, and whose bronze fittings look like a flattened brutalist sculpture with two projecting rocket launchers, forms the roof of the club. From above it looks like a helicopter pad. Reflective plates open up to the night

Bernard Khoury's bad-boy nightclub (Beatrice Teissier)

sky displaying lights and revellers and propelling the sound outwards. In his 2009 lecture 'New Wars in Progress' Khoury stated that he is against the sugar coating of history and sees his work in terms of devices responding to real context, not as metaphors.[43] This club is one of Beirut's most celebrated, and one of its preferred gay venues.

The atmosphere of Karantina also attracted visceral street art and graffiti (now mostly erased or wiped out) such as 'We burn it' by Otaiby and 'Freedom will never come for free' by M'alim.[44] Art galleries like the Sfeir-Semler, severely damaged during the explosion and set in the industrial Tannous building, specialized in conceptual art by Arab artists of all ages (from Etel Adnan to Akram Zaatani) and in November 2021 was showing a retrospective of the works of Aref el Rayers, a Lebanese artist particularly well-known between the 1960s and 1980s. The now closed Art Factum Gallery similarly showed contemporary art.

The cobbling together by locals of what was left of Karantina after the tragedy of 4 August 2020 shows who the true phoenixes of this scarred but resilient city are.

1 Khalaf 1998, 157.
2 ibid, 157.
3 Khoder, *L'Orient le Jour* 2010.
4 Debbas 1986, 187-191; Kassir 2011, 188, 221.
5 Saliba 2009, 67, 74-77.
6 Tabet 1998, figs. 16, 17; blfheadquarters.com.
7 Zantout 2018, 178-179.
8 ibid, 198.
9 *Daily Star*, 2017.
10 Kassir 2011, 126; Rayes Ingea 2018, 11.
11 Bodenstein 2007, 203; Rayes Ingea 2018, 18-19, 22.
12 https://sursockhouse.com
13 Rayes Ingea 2018, 32-33.
14 The Arab Center for Architecture in Mar Mitr has occasional tours.
15 Rayes Ingea 2018, 26-27.
16 Saliba 2009, 43.
17 Bodenstein 2007, 204.
18 Bodenstein 2007, 204-239, Abb. 233, 234.
19 YouTube, 'Quick Take: Beirut Blast: Landmark Sursock Palace Seriously Damaged.'
20 Makarem 2020, *L'Orient le Jour*, Rayes Ingea.
21 Bodenstein 2007, 207-208.
22 Gardner, Architectural Digest 2017.
23 Camille Tarazi, personal communication.
24 Tarazi 2015, 118.
25 Camille Tarazi, personal communication.
26 Tarazi 2015, 202-203.
27 ibid, 280-281.
28 www.albawaba.Terazi 2020.
29 Debbas 1986, 177, 179.
30 Davie 2007, paras 3, 11.
31 ibid, paras 13-16, figs 6-7.
32 ibid, para 18.
33 ibid, para 20.
34 ibid, para 13.
35 ibid, fig 9.
36 ibid, paras 23-27.
37 Sewell, *L'Orient Today*, 2 August 2021.
38 e.g. Port City Futures 2021.
39 Kassir 2011, 296.
40 Fisk 1992, 73-79, 99.
41 Arsan 2018, 195.
42 ibid, 373.
43 stamps.umich.edu.video
44 Zantout 2018, 28, 37.

# APPENDIX
# A BRIEF ARCHITECTURAL
# OVERVIEW

## Potpourri

In the early nineteenth century the Beirut cityscape consisted largely of flat-roofed stone houses of one or two storeys, with mostly rectangular windows and a few arcaded spaces. Mid-century onwards, pitched roofs and imported red tiles (from France) and the triple arcaded central bay (which came to define later nineteenth- and early twentieth-century domestic architecture) became characteristic of bourgeois houses. But it was from the 1860s, in conjunction with the economic growth of Beirut, that one of the most dynamic periods in the history of its architecture was initiated. It saw the expansion of public and educational buildings, and the proliferation of multi-storey apartment buildings, villas and mansions in a variety of eclectic styles (neo-Islamic or neo-Ottoman, Moorish, Egyptianizing, Haussmann Parisian, Italianate, Baronial) influenced by Paris, Istanbul and other *fin-de-siècle* cities like Alexandria and locally adapted. From the 1920s, Art Nouveau and Art Deco styles were added to the mix and from 1930 modernism appeared.

The series of monumental civic buildings which defined late Ottoman Beirut were the Grand Serail (1853-1894), the Petit Serail (1884-1888, demolished); the Orosdi-Back department store (1880s, demolished) and the Hamidiye clocktower (1897-98). The Syrian Protestant College (later AUB, 1866), and the Jesuit Université de St Joseph (1883) founded at this period reflected American Gothic campus architecture and a French colonial style respectively. The Prussian Deaconesses' School (1862) was more Italianate, with semi-circular arches and oculi.

Imported materials such as concrete (made locally from 1930), cast iron (from England), roof tiles (France) and Lebanese moulded cemento floor tiles with geometric patterns, facilitated eclecticism. This was particularly evident in domestic

Mandate-period tiles from the Lebanese Fine Arts Institute
(Beatrice Teissier)

architecture, which became extravagant in the hands of the elite bourgeoisie who could afford imported goods and master craftsmen with foreign apprenticeships in Istanbul or Tuscany for their mansions in areas like Zokak el Blat and Sursock. This led to a medley of styles, both interior and exterior (fantastical central bays and openings, elaborate staircases, turrets, coloured glass etc.). The interior eclecticism of these mansions is repeated nowadays in their restoration, with modern imports such as Czech chandeliers, modern Italian furniture, international and Islamic art objects.

The use of concrete and cast concrete, replacing the local sandstone, also encouraged the development of multi-storey apartments for the lower middle class, with different levels of decoration, from cast blocks made to resemble stonework or mouldings around doorways, to cast concrete balustrades or projecting, sometimes rounded verandahs supported by rounded or square pillars and recessed central bays. Triple arched central bays were used as entrances and/or on the upper floors as window or balcony bays, usually framed by rectangular windows, and this dominant feature also engendered other developments such as bow windows and verandahs. The original points of the triple arch, derived from the vernacular *liwan* (vaulted porch) and subsequently joined with side windows under European influence, was first replaced by other forms (semi-circular, horseshoe, segmented, chamfered, rectangle) until, under the influence of modernism, the whole bay became rectangular. Characteristic of balconies were wrought-iron balustrades showing a great variety of styles, from plain geometric to Art Nouveau and Art Deco. Concrete also dominated the plain rectangular apartment blocks built for the working classes.

The pioneering architects of these revivalist eclectic styles in the early twentieth century were the foreign-trained or foreign-influenced architect-engineers Bishara Affendi (Petit Serail,

Sanayeh Complex, Ottoman Bank), Yussuf Aftimus (Barakat Building, 1924, Hamidiye clocktower, Beirut City Hall 1933); Bishara Deeb, working with Aftimus, and Mardiros Altounian (Beirut Parliament, 1931, Abed clocktower, 1934) aided by master-craftsmen.

It has been argued that the Islamicist revival styles, popular with both the Muslim and the Christian bourgeoisie, were merely copied and diluted by local architects and never produced an integrated local version. Nor did they engender a local reaction to this essentially European inspired eclecticism.[1] Yet the variety and originality of these styles, as well as their common aesthetic, despite later additions, remains harmonious in present-day Beirut in contrast with much of what came later.

**Massive and brutal**

By the 1930s a modernist, sometimes brutalist, trend emerged side by side with the earlier eclectic styles, and the city became increasingly defined by individual architects (again foreign- or partly foreign-trained) building showpieces in defiance of 'colonial' styles. It was the beginning of another kind of eclecticism, leaping across genres: from Art Deco/ New York statements (Charles Corm, 1926-29) to brutalism. The cohesion of the *fin-de-siècle* and early twentieth-century architecture had been broken, and the era of the cult of the architect-engineer and architects' firms had begun. This architecture was defined by the use of reinforced concrete and simple, rectangular, block-like, sometimes monumental forms, with few classical references. Pioneers of this style were Farid Trad (Unesco building, Palais de Justice) and Antoine Tabet (St George Hotel 1930-32), followed by George Rayes, Theo Kanaan and Karl Chayer in the 1950s. Elevators introduced in the 1940s intensified the exploitation of space.

This architecture, despite the influence of Bauhaus and German Expressionists, arguably reinterpreted foreign models to become local.[2] This is something only architects are able to detect and support: the concept of local identity is much exercised in discussions of Lebanese architecture, with greater or lesser persuasiveness (see further). The 1960s has been called the 'Golden Age' of Lebanese architecture, and there was certainly a building boom. Commissions, again to foreign and foreign-trained architects, were given and competitions launched. This led to the creation of functional buildings under the partial influence of Le Corbusier: Joseph Philippe Karam, apartment building in Raouche, 1962; Pierre Neema and Jacques Aractingi, Électricité du Liban, 1966; the Japanese School (Khoury Building, Spears Street), but also of more lyrical examples (Neema and Aractingi, Maison de l'Artisan, 1966, with modernist arches now covered with another façade, supporting a flat roof, Corniche), which referenced tradition.

Tradition was also more distantly referenced in, for example, the building of the Khashoggi Mosque in the Horsch area (Assem Salam), with the use of sandstone but in a geometric building, with the dome transformed into the Islamic eight-pointed star, and the traditionally round minaret into a square 'campanile'. Notorious buildings of the 1960-1970s were, for example, The Egg (Joseph Philippe Karam, 1965, unfinished); the Koujak-Jaber building (Victor Bisharat, 1967); the Holiday Inn (Andre Wogensky, Maurice Hindie, 1971-74); the Phoenicia (American and local architects, 1961); the Shell Building (Karl Shayer, Wassek Adib, 1962). Unfortunately, this period's mixed use buildings aided by *laissez-faire* town planning often led to a dull corporate style.

## Shambolic

The civil war (1975-1990) and subsequent Israeli attacks caused much destruction to Beirut and its infrastructure, first in the central area, which became a type of no-man's land, then to the periphery as battles extended to the port, the airport and beyond. It was not a time to launch building projects, even though reconstruction did occur, and the reconstruction of the centre was already mooted in the late 1970s and 1980s. The real estate company Solidère gained a monopoly over this project with the collusion of the government, and the plan was formally approved in 1992. President Rafik Hariri was the major shareholder.

Amidst this massive endeavour to construct and reconstruct the centre, roads, highways and underpasses, interest in Beirut real estate flourished, and foreign and corporate ownership, allied with legal exemptions from planning regulations, produced and continued to produce building booms until 2019. This has created a spectrum of modern 'polymorphous' and 'polychromatic' styles, partly in reaction to the plain, brutalist styles of the pre-war period (although these are still being produced, see below).

In terms of function, many buildings incorporate business, leisure and residential premises. High-end ones have penthouses, garden roof terraces, swimming pools, gyms. Huge tower blocks can be plain and rectangular, semi-circular, have chequered façades, block-like protrusions, be ziggurat-shaped and have different finishes: basalt, sandstone, exposed concrete, glass. The balcony can be an external feature as before (box-like, rectangular, flat) or can be swallowed up by the architecture, but all façades have to take into account heat and light, so have different, sometimes moveable, sunscreen systems (meshed, louvred, wooden panels).

There are a number of prominent local architects and architect firms in Beirut: Bernard Khoury, B018 nightclub, 1998; Maroun Daccache, Risveglio office building, 2005; Nabil Gholam. Foch 94, 2004, Engineering Complex, AUB, 2012.

Bernard Khoury's towering Plot #450 (Beatrice Teissier)

But a foreign name and reputation perhaps has even more cachet today than it ever did as in the case of Rafael Moneo with Samir Khairalla, the southern souks, and Zaha Hadid's 'fishnet' building under construction in the city centre.

The common narrative in the promotion of such inventive modern buildings is that they respond to their urban surroundings and the climate, using local materials. The reality is that few such buildings are, or can be, integrated into their immediate surroundings, and are rather completely divorced from them, like statements of self-sufficiency or as if courting a *succès de scandale*. They contribute to eradicating Beirut's sense of place. This does not mean that architecturally some these building are not pleasing (e.g. the Campus of Innovation and Sports at USJ), although some are universally disliked such as the 195-metre Sama tower, the highest in Beirut, or the landscape sabotaging Issam Fares Institute building in the AUB campus. Here again reliance on famous names (Zaha Hahid architects for the latter) seems to justify anything. Other developments, attempting a more 'traditional' style, like the Saifi Village in the centre, can appear harmonious or kitsch depending on one's taste, but again seem marooned.

In conjunction with gated communities and luxurious shopping malls such multi-million-dollar apartments and office spaces only enhance a sense of exclusiveness and separation, and are light years away from the concrete terraced habitations of ordinary people. To those who are not architects, the language of modern architecture in Beirut seems to be primarily addressed to, and understood by, other architects: it continues to shock and challenge, but often in ways which offend rather than inspire the eye, while having lost any meaningful concept of local identity. We have yet to see what will emerge from the post-port explosion period.

1   Saliba 1998, 145.
2   Tabet 1998, 93.

# BIBLIOGRAPHY

Abu Hodeib, T. 2017 *A Taste for Home: the Modern Middle Class in Ottoman Beirut*. Stanford: Stanford University Press

Aghacy, S. 2015 *Writing Beirut, Mappings of the City in the Modern Arabic Novel*. Edinburgh: Edinburgh University Press

Arsan, A. 2018 *Lebanon: A Country in Fragments*. London: Hurst

Ayalou, A. 2018 *The Arabic Print Revolution, Cultural Production and Mass Readership*. Cambridge: Cambridge University Press

Badre, L. 1997 'Bey 003 Preliminary Report: Excavations of the American University of Beirut Museum', *Baal* 2, 6-94/ 2000 'Recently Discovered Bronze Age Temples: Middle Bronze Beirut and Late Bronze Tell Kazel' in *Proceedings of the First International Congress on the Archaeology of the Ancient Near East*, May 1998, vol. I. Rome: Universita degli Studi di Roma, La Sapienza.

2016 The Greek Orthodox Cathedral of Saint George in Beirut, Lebanon: The Archaeological Excavations and Crypt Museum in researchgate.net (also in *Journal of Eastern Mediterranean Archaeology and Heritage Studies*, 4/1, 72-97)

Battah, H. 2018-19 'Race against time: how luxury developers are wiping out ancient Beirut', www.beirutreport.com

Baedeker, K. 1876 *Handbook for Travellers to Palestine and Syria*. London.

Baghdadi, L.M. 2013 Lesbanon: the Lesbian Experience in Lebanon, MA thesis, Georgetown University, euromedwomen. foundation

Bayoumi, N. 2014 'Femininity and feminist Studies: Research, the Researcher and Cultural Constrictions in Lebanon', in *Arab feminisms: Gender and Equality in the middle East*, eds. J. Makdisi, N. Bayoumi, 90-107. London: I.B. Tauris

Berchet, J-C. ed. 1985 *Le Voyage en Orient*. Paris: Robert Laffont

Blondel, E. 1838 'A Difficult Landing', in *A Beirut Anthology*, ed. T.J. Gorton 2015, 35-36

Bodenstein, R. 2005 'The Making and Remaking of Zokak el-Blat: the History of the Urban Fabric', in *History, Space and Social Conflict in Beirut, the Quarter of Zokak el Blat*. Würzbürg-Beirut: Ergon Verlag

2012 *Villen in Beirut, Wohnkultur und sozialer Wandel 1860-1930*. Petersberg: Michael Imhof Verlag

Brones, S. 2012 'The Beit Beirut Project: Heritage Practices and the Barakat Building' *in Archives, Museums and Collecting Practices in the Modern Arab World*, eds. S. Mejcher-Atassi and J.P. Swartz: London, New York: Routledge

Charaf, H. 2018 'The Northern Levant (Lebanon) during the Middle Bronze Age' in *The Oxford Handbook of the Archaeology of the Levant c. 8000-332B.C.*, eds. M.L. Steiner and A.F. Killerbrew, 434-450

Chognot, J-P. 2010 'L'immeuble de l'Orient, un trésor architectural et historique bientôt restauré' www.lorientlejour.com

Curvers, H. and Stuart, B. 2016 'Beirut Archaeological Heritage Management (1993-2015): A metaphor of text and theatre', in *Berytus* 55, 263-291

Curvers, H. 2017 'Soundings, Contexts and Sequences', in *Der Hippodrome von Berytos (2012-2015), Marburger Winckleman Programm 2015-2016*, Marburg: Phillips Universität, Archaeologischen Seminars Verlag

Daher, J. 206 *Hezbollah*. London: Pluto Press

Davie, M. 1984 'Trois cartes inédites de Beyrouth: éléments cartographiques pour une histoire urbaine de la ville', *Annales de Géographie de l'Université de St. Joseph* 5, 37-82

Davie, M. 2003 'Genèse d'une maison patrimoniale: la maison aux Trois Arcs de Beyrouth', in *La Maison Beyrouthine aux Trois Arcs, une Architecture Bourgeoise de Levant*. M.F. Davie ed., Académie Libanaise des Beaux-Arts: Beirut, 57-96

2007 'Saint Dimitri, un cimitière orthodoxe de Beyrouth', in *Annales de Bretagne et des Pays de l'Ouest*, 114, or http/alopo.revues.org/457

del Castillo, D. 2000 'Cemeteries: history's final resting place', *Daily Star* (August) Beirut

Elayi, J. 2010 'An Unexpected Archaeological Treasure: the Phoenician Quarters in Beirut City Centre', *Near Eastern Archaeology* 73/2, 156-168

Eliseef, N. 1960 'Bayrūt', *The Encyclopaedia of Islam* vol.1, Leiden: Brill, 1137-1138

Eyrad, J.P and Krebs, G. 2007 *Le Protestantisme Français et le Levant (de 1865 à nos jours)*, Strasbourg: Oberlin

Fisk, R. 1992/2001 (3rd ed.) *Pity the Nation: Lebanon at War*, Oxford: Oxford University Press

2016 'Restoring Beirut's Pink House is a cheering idea amid destruction' @indy.voices

Gardner, A. 2017 'Look inside May Daouk's Eclectic 19th century Villa in Lebanon', www.architecturaldigest.com

Gebara, H.K. 2016 Tactical Urbanism and the Restoration of Residual Spaces: Reviving Ain Mresseih's Socio-Cultural heritage, MA thesis, AUB, Beirut

Goodchild, T.J. 2000 'Oxbridge's Tudor Gothic Influences on American Academic Architecture', *Paedagogica Historica* 36/1, 266-298, Taylor-Francis Online

Gorton T.J. and A.C. Gorton eds. 2009 *Lebanon through Writers' Eyes*, London: Eland

Gorton, T.J. 2014 *Renaissance Emir, A Druze Warlord at the Court of the Medici*, Northampton MA: Olive Branch Press

2015 ed. *A Beirut Anthology*, Cairo/New York: AU Cairo Press

Hage, R. 2015 'Bird Nation', in *Beirut Noir*, ed. I. Humaydan, Brooklyn: Akaschic Books, 113-118

Hammel, E.M. 1985 *The Root: the Marines in Beirut, August 1982-February 1983*. New York: Harcourt Brace Jovanovich

Hanssen, J. 1998 'Your Beirut is on my desk', Ottomanizing Beirut under Sultan Abdulhamid II (1876-1909)', in *Projecting Beirut, Episodes in the Construction and Reconstruction of a Modern City*, eds. P. Rowe and H. Sarkis, Munich, London, New York: Prestel, 41-67

2005a *Fin de Siècle Bierut: the Making of an Ottoman Provincial Capital*, Oxford: Oxford University Press

2005b 'The Birth of an Education Quarter: Zokak el Blat as a Cradle of Cultural Revival in the Arab World', in *History, Space and Social Conflict in Beirut*. Orient-Institut Beirut, Würzbürg: Ergon Verlag, 143-174

Hanssen, J. and Genberg, D. 2001 'Beirut in Memoriam', in *Crisis and Memory in Islamic Societies*, ed. A. Neuwirth, Würzbürg: Ergon Verlag, 231-262

Hardy, R. 2018 *The Poisoned Well*. London: Hurst

al Harithy, H. 2008 'Weaving historical narratives: Beirut's Last Mamluk Monument', *Muqarnas* 25, 215-230

Harris, W. 2012 *Lebanon: a History 600-2011*. Oxford: Oxford University Press

Hayek, G. 2015 and 2020 *Beirut, Imagining the City, Space and Place in Lebanese Literature*. London: Bloomsbury-I.B. Tauris

Herztein, R. 2015 'The Oriental Library and the Catholic Press at St. Joseph University in Beirut', *Journal of Jesuit Studies*, 2/2, 248-264

Hill, P. 2020 *Utopia and Civilization in the Arab Nahda*. Cambridge: Cambridge University Press

Hillenkamp, B. 2005 'From the Margins to the Centre? Kurds and Shiites in a changing Zokak el Blat in West Beirut', in *History, Space and Social Conflict in Beirut*. Orient-Institut Beirut, Würzbürg: Ergon Verlag, 213-245

Hindi, N. 2016 'Recurrent Warscape in Beirut Public Spaces: Forty Years Later (1975-2015), in *History, Urbanism, Resilience, Planning and Heritage* 17/4, journal.open.tudelft.nl, 1-10

Ibrahim, I. ed. 2020 *Beyrouth Mon Amour*. Lebanon: Al Arz Printing Press

Jacobs, D.L. 2013 'Postcards from Beirut: Preservationists Lose Battle to Save Historic Buildings from Bulldozer', www.forbes.com

Jaubert, P.A. 1824 *Géographie d'Edrisi, Recueil des Voyages et de Mémoires* 5. Paris: Imprimerie Royale

Jones Hall, L 2004 and 2008 *Roman Berytus, Beirut in Late Antiquity*. Abingdon: Routledge

Jureidini, P., McLaurin R.D., Price J. '1979 Military Operations in Selected Lebanese Built Up Areas'. US Army Human Engineering Lab., Technical Memorandum, Aberdeen: M.D., 11-79

Kahlenberg, C. 2019 *The Star of David in a Cedar Tree: Jewish Students and Zionism at the American University of Beirut (1908-1948)*. Taylor and Francis online

Karam, K. 2016 'Beirut's Old Manara'. 365daysoflebanon.com

Kassir, S. 1994 *La guerre du Liban; de la dissention nationale au conflit régional (1975-1982)*. Karthata-Cermac: Paris

2011 *Beirut*. Los Angeles, London: University of California Press

Kaufmann, A. 2014 *Reviving Phoenicia, the Search for Identity in Lebanon*. New York: I.B. Tauris

Khalaf, S. 1998 'Contested Space and the Forging of New Cultural Identities', in *Projecting Beirut*. eds. P. Rowe and H. Sarkis. Munich, London, New York: Prestel, 140-164

2002 *Civil and Uncivil Violence*. New York: Columbia University Press

2006 *Heart of Beirut, Reclaiming the Bourj*. London: Saqi

Khalaf, S. and P. Kongstad 1973 *Hamra of Beirut: A Case of Rapid Urbanization*. Leiden: Brill

Khalidi, R. 2007 'The Palestinians and 1948; the underlying causes of failure', in *The War for Palestine*, 2nd ed. 12-36. eds. E. Rogan and A. Schlaim. Cambridge: Cambridge University Press

Khoder, P. 2010 'Les 175 ans de l'École des Trois Docteurs', *L'Orient le Jour* (May)

Knusden, A.J. and Gade, T. eds. 2017 'The Lebanese Armed Forces (LAF): a united army for a divided country', in *Civil-Military Relations in Lebanon: conflict, cohesion and confessionalism in a divided society*. 1-22. Cham, Switzerland: Palgrave Macmillan.

Kögler, O. 2005 'Prospects for Preservation of Historic Buildings' in *History, Space and Social Conflict in Beirut, the Quarter of Zokak el Blat*. Orient-Institut Beirut. Würzbürg: Ergon Verlag, 261-288

Krijnen, M. and de Beukelaer, C. 2015 'Capital, State and Conflict: the various drivers of diverse gentrification processes in Beirut, Lebanon', in *Global Gentrifications: Uneven Development and Displacement*, eds. L. Lees et al. Bristol: Policy Press, 285-309

Lamartine, A. 1835 *Voyage en Orient* extracts taken from *Le Voyage en Orient*, 1985. ed. J-C Berchet. Paris: Robert Laffont, 710-741

Lammens, H. 1921 *La Syrie: Précis historique*. 2 vols. Beyrouth: Imprimerie Catholique

Levesque, C. 2014 'Welcome to Bachoura, or the Found City as Interstice', in *Terrain Vague, Interstices at the Edge of the Pale*, eds. M. Mariani, P. Barron. Montreal: Routledge

Lyckberg, P. 2013 'The MIM Museum Opening', www.mindat.org

McCarthy K.M. 1975 'Street Names in Beirut, Lebanon', *Names* 23/2, 74-88

MacIntyre, B. 2014 *A Spy Among Friends, Philby and the Great Betrayal*. London: Bloomsbury

MacMillan 1905 *Guide to Syria and Palestine*. London: MacMillan and Co.

Majdalani, C. 2020 *Beirut 2020, the Collapse of a Civilization*. R. Driver trans. Welbeck-London: Mountain Leopard Press

Makarem, M. 2020 'The Rebirth of La Maison Rayes in Sursock Street', https://today.lorientlejour.com

Mattar, P. 1988 *The Mufti of Jerusalem, Al-Hajj Amin al-Husayni and the Palestinian National Movement*. New York: Columbia University Press

Merabet, S. 2014 *Queer Beirut*. Austin: University of Texas Press

Mikati, R. and Perring, D. 2006 'From Metropolis to Ribat, some recent work on Beirut at the end of antiquity', *Archaeology and History in the Lebanon* 23, 42-55

Mezher, N. 2021 'Lignes de ruptures, interactions et territorialité dans l'espace public à Beyrouth', *African and Mediterranean Journal of Architecture and Urbanism*, 5, 1-19

Mikati, R. 2013 The Creation of Early Islamic Beirut: the Sea, Scholars, Jihad and the Sacred. DPhil thesis, Chicago University, Chicago IL. My thanks to H. Curvers for this reference

Mikesell, M.W. 1969 'The Deforestation of Mt. Lebanon'. *Geographical Review* 59, 1-28.

Mollenhauser, A. 2005 'Continuity and Change in the Architectural Development of Zokak el Blat, in *History, Space and Social Conflict in Beirut, the Quarter of Zokak el Blat*. Orient-Institut Beirut. Würzbürg: Ergon Verlag, 109-142

Murray, J. 1858 *Murray's Handbook for Travellers in Syria and Palestine*. London: John Murray

Naccache, A. 1998 'Beirut's Memorycide, Hear no Evil, See no Evil', in *Archaeology under Fire: Nationalism, Politics and Heritage in the Eastern Mediterranean and the Middle East*. ed. L. Meskell. London: Routledge, 140-158

Nahle, R. 2021 'Activating public life in Neighbourhoods through Soft Mobility and a Network of Open Spaces, the Case of Badaro', Beirut Infrastructure. MUD Thesis, Faculty of Engineering and Design, American University of Beirut

Najjar, Z. 2015 'Beirut Street Art: Caught in the Crossfire'. www.middleasteye.net

Oweini, A. 1969 'Stress and Coping: the Experience of Students at the American University of Beirut during the Lebanese Civil War', *Arab Studies Quarterly* 18, 69-90

Papkova, I. 2016 'The Three Religions of Armenians in Lebanon', in *Armenian Christianity Today: Identity Politics and Popular Practice*. London, New York: Routledge, 171-196

Philby, K. 1967 *My Silent War, the Autobiography of a Spy*. London: Random House

Quinn, J. 2018 *In Search of the Phoenicians*. New Jersey, Oxford: Princeton University Press

Raidy, G. 2017 'Yazan Halwani immortalises West Beirut Movie in a Gorgeous Mural on the Former Green Line', ginosblog.com

Rayes Ingea, T. 2018 *Portraits et Palais, Récit de famille autour de Victor et Helène Sursock*. Beirut: Private publication.

Renan, E. 1864 *Mission de Phénicie*. Paris: Imprimerie Royale

Sader, H. 1998 'Ancient Beirut: Urban Growth in the Light of Recent Excavations', in *Projecting Beirut, Episodes in the Construction and Reconstruction of a Modern City*. eds. P. Rowe and H. Sarkis. Munich, London, New York: Prestel 23-40

2001 'Lebanon's Heritage, Will the Past be Part of the Future?', in *Crisis and Memory in Islamic Societies*. eds. A. Neuwirth and A. Pflitsch. Beirut: Ergon Verlag, 217-262

2016 'Between Looters and Private Collectors: the Tragic Fate of Lebanese Antiquities', in *Archives, Museums and Collecting*

*Practices in the Modern Arab World.* eds. S. Mercher-Atassi and J.P. Swartz. London, New York: Routledge, 57-70

2019 *The History and Archaeology of Phoenicia.* Atlanta: SBL Press

Saliba, R. 1997 'The Mental Image of Downtown Beirut, 1990', in *Beyrouth: regards croisés.* ed. M.F. Davie, Tours: Urbama, 307-349

2004 *Beirut City Centre Recovery-The Foch-Allenby and Étoile Conservation.* Beirut: Steidl

2009 *Beyrouth, architectures aux sources de la modernité.* Marseille: Editions Parenthèses.

Sawalha, A. 2010 *Reconstructing Beirut: Memory and Space in a Post-War Arab City.* Austin: University of Texas Press

Schlaim, A. 2007 'Israel and the Arab Coalition in 1948', in *The War for Palestine.* eds. E. Rogan and A. Schlaim. Cambridge: Cambridge University Press, 79-103

Schulze, K.E. 2009 *The Jews in Lebanon: Between Coexistence and Conflict.* Eastbourne: Sussex Academic Press

Schwairi, S.T. 2008 'From Regional Node to Backwater and Back to Uncertainty: Beirut 1943-2006', in *The Evolving Arab City, Tradition, Modernity and Urban Development.* ed. Y. Esheshtawy. Abingdon: Routledge, 69-98

Sewell, A. 2021 'Holding Bay, refuge, dumping ground, home, war zone, community: the storied past of blast-devastated Karantina', *L'Orient le Jour* 2 August 2021

Sheehy, S. 2011 'Butrus-Bustani, Syria's Idealogue of the Age', in *The Origins of Syrian Nationhood, Histories, pioneers and identity.* ed. A. Beshara. London, New York: Routledge 57-78

El-Solh, N. 2021 *The P.M.'s Beirut Mansion. If Walls Could Speak...* London: Unicorn

Stolleis, F. 2005 'The Inhabitants of Zokak el-Blat, Demographic Shifts and Patterns of Interaction, in *History, Space and Social Conflict*, Orient-Institut Beirut, Würzburg: Ergon Verlag

Stoughton, I. 2018 'Piece in the Middle East: Famous Sculpture Symbolising Non-Violence Unveiled in Beirut'. www.the nationalnews.com

Stuart, B. and Curvers, H. 2014 'Cemeteries in Beirut' in Round Table on Mortuary Customs in Beled Sham. DAAD and University of Amman, Jordan, 1-34

Tabet, J. 1998 'From Colonial Style to Regional Revivalism: Modern Architecture in Lebanon and the Problem of Cultural Identity', in *Projecting Beirut: Episodes in the Construction and Reconstruction of a Modern City*. eds. P. Rowe and H. Sarkis. Munich, London, New York: Prestel, 83-105

Tahan, L. 2014 'Challenging Museum Spaces: Dancing with Ethnic and Cultural Diversity in Lebanon', in *The Politics and Practices of Cultural Heritage in the Middle East*, eds. R. Daher and I. Maffi, 135-147

Talty, A. 2013 'Postcards from Beirut: Preservationists Lose Battle to Save Historic Building from Bulldozer'. www.forbes.com

Tarazi, C. with T. Reas-Ingea 2015 *Vitrine de l'Orient: Maison Tarazi, fondée à Beyrouth en 1862*. Beirut: Editions de la Revue Phénicienne

Trablousi, F. 2012 *A History of Modern Lebanon*. New York: Pluto Press

Vloeberghs, W. 2015 *Architecture, Power and Religion in Lebanon: Rafiq Hariri and the Politics of Sacred Space in Beirut*. Leiden: Brill

Young, T. c.2017-18 *Lost Levantine Houses of Beirut* www.tomyoung. /www.levantineheritage.com

Volk, L. 2010 *Memorials and Martyrs in Modern Lebanon*. Bloomington IN: Indiana University Press

Zachs, F. 2011 'Pioneers of Syrian Patriotism and Identity: A re-valuation of Khalil al-Khuri's Contribution', in *The Origins of Syrian Nationhood: Histories, Pioneers and Identity*. ed. A. Beshara. London, New York: Routledge, 91-107

Zamir, M. 2005 'An Intimate Alliance: the Joint Struggle of General Edward Spears and Riad al Sulh to Oust France from Lebanon 1942-1944'. *Middle Eastern Studies* 41/6, 811-832

Zantout, T. 2018 *Drawing Lines*. Beirut: Urban Fusion.

# ACKNOWLEDGEMENTS

I AM GREATLY INDEBTED TO the following who contributed, whether virtually or in person, to the making of this book: Claudine Abdelmassih, Umit Firat Acikgoz, Anne-Marie Maila Afeiche, George Arbid, Andrew Arsan, Maya Boustani, Mona Fawaz, Rowina Bou-Harb, Mona Harb, Hans Curvers, Salma Dalmuji, Hayat Gebara, Alain George, Helene Sader, Camille Terazi. My warmest thanks to Jamaila Chaccour and Mira Khfoury for our joint explorations, to Alex and Hiam Fallaha and the families of Ibrahim Najem and Jamaila Chaccour for their hospitality and to Ahmed (Ain el Mreisseh), Bob (Hamra) and all the other people in the street who were willing to stop and talk. I am especially grateful to the many scholars and journalists whose research I have used in the writing of this book, and in particular to the seminal works of Samir Kassir and Robert Fisk. All mistakes are mine. Last but certainly not least, I would like to warmly thank my editor James Ferguson and the map designer Stephanie Ferguson.

# INDEX